# CUMULATIVE ADVANTAGE

How to Build Momentum for Your Ideas,
Business, and Life *Against All Odds*

# MARK W. SCHAEFER

This publication is designed to provide accurate and authoritative information in regard to the subject matter covered. It is sold with the understanding that neither the author nor the publisher is engaged in rendering legal, accounting, or other professional service. If legal advice or other expert assistance is required, the services of a competent professional person should be sought. - From a Declaration of Principles jointly adopted by a Committee of the American Bar Association and a Committee of Publishers.

Schaefer Marketing Solutions

www.businessesGROW.com

First Edition: February 2021

Publisher is not responsible for websites (or their content) that are not owned by the publisher.

Library of Congress Cataloging-in-Publication Data

Schaefer, Mark W.

Cumulative Advantage: How to Build Momentum for Your Ideas, Life, and Business Against All Odds

Mark W. Schaefer - 1st ed.

ISBN-13: 978-1-7335533-5-3

*To the Parker Family, who taught me the meaning of courage and momentum, against all odds.*

# OTHER BOOKS BY MARK W. SCHAEFER

*The Tao of Twitter, Changing Your Life and Your Business One Tweet at a Time*

*Return On Influence, The Power of Influencer Marketing*

*Born to Blog (with Stanford Smith)*

*Social Media Explained*

*The Content Code, Six Essential Strategies to Ignite Your Content, Your Marketing, and Your Business*

*KNOWN, The Handbook to Build and Unleash Your Personal Brand in the Digital Age*

*Marketing Rebellion: The Most Human Company Wins*

# CONTENTS

# INTRODUCTION

Tim Ferriss knows Oprah.

I do not.

The underlying purpose of this book is to figure out why.

Understanding how Tim launched his career into Oprah Orbit—and why I did not—has implications for the momentum of YOUR ideas, business, and career.

Significant implications, by the way.

If you don't recognize his name, Tim Ferriss is one of the most renowned authors and self-help gurus on the globe.

His first book, *The 4-Hour Workweek: Escape 9-5, Live Anywhere and Join the New Rich*, was a sensation that spent more than four years on the *New York Times* Best Seller List and has sold more than 2.1 million copies worldwide.

The success of the book propelled Tim into the glittery echelon of celebrity, and today, everything he touches turns to gold.

- His podcast has topped 500 million downloads with 9,000 five-star reviews.
- He's one of the highest-paid speakers in the world at $75,000 per appearance.
- CNN named him "one of the planet's leading angel investors."
- He's written four more books, all instant best sellers.

Tim Ferriss is Mr. Success, a hero to a generation looking to hack a lifestyle that gets more life out of less work.

Yes ... it's good to be Tim Ferriss.

I was curious to learn how Tim generated the momentum to become the star he is today, so I snooped around. He's been quite open about his history—transparency is part of Tim's charm. Here are a few highlights from my investigation:

- Ferriss was born prematurely in Long Island, NY. He was small for his age and bullied as a child.
- In an interview, he said he grew up nerdy, hyperactive, and prone to serious health problems.[1]
- He lived in a middle-class home, but his parents would buy him as many books as he wanted, nurturing a love of reading.
- He graduated from college with a degree in East Asian Studies after completing a senior thesis entitled

"Acquisition of Japanese Kanji: Conventional Practice and Mnemonic Supplementation." (I have no idea what that means.)

- After graduation, Tim worked in sales at a data storage company.

- In a famous TED talk (with 8 million views), he openly discussed a suicide attempt during his college years, battles with bipolar depression, and self-paralysis that prevented him from following through on much of anything.

- He hit another low in 2004 after a friend died, a long-term relationship ended, and his business startup stalled despite the many hours he put into it. He took a year off, traveled Europe, and collected ideas for a book.

- His pitch for *The 4-Hour Workweek* (originally titled *Drug Dealing for Fun and Profit*) was rejected by 26 different publishers.

After learning all these facts, I was disappointed. There's just not a lot here that would have foreshadowed his astronomical success.

Even after his book took off like a comet, many of the reviews were scathing. Some thought Ferriss was recycling old self-help techniques, exploiting technicalities in sometimes unethical and dishonorable ways (he admittedly likes to cheat), and that his success was due in large part to his considerable skills as a self-promoter.

The fact that Tim Ferriss is an A-list luminary is so improbable ... and that's exactly what makes him an irresistible case study. When you examine where he was in his life up until the age of 29 (when he wrote his book), predicting he would soon be hobnobbing with stars like Hugh Jackman and LeBron James would confound even the most aggressive Las Vegas oddsmakers.

Clearly *something crazy* happened.

"Nobody expected the book to be a success," Tim said in an interview. "It had an initial print run of like 10,000 copies, which isn't even *partial* national distribution. But I think the timing was right, and to everybody's amazement, including my own, it became the number one *New York Times* best seller."

Then, the Tim Ferriss Hit Machine really revved up.

- The book's success enabled new relationships with top venture capitalists who taught him the insider secrets of investing.
- Based on this advice, he built a multi-million-dollar investment portfolio that included more than 50 companies like Shopify, Evernote, and Uber.
- His new wealth and book-fame rocketed him into orbit with leaders in business, sports, and entertainment.
- He leveraged these dazzling new connections to create a star-filled podcast with eager sponsors.

- Tim then took these podcast interviews and pieced them together into another best-selling book called *Tribe of Mentors*, filled with stories from celebrities such as Arianna Huffington, Madeleine Albright, and Neil deGrasse Tyson.

I need to pause the Tim Ferriss Success Fest for a moment to compare and contrast his career trajectory with my own. It makes a point, I assure you. In fact, it makes THE point of this book.

Tim and I published our first books at roughly the same time. From this "starting line," I had more than twice as much business experience than Tim, more education (including three years studying under the world-famous management consultant Peter Drucker), and I had a larger audience (500 percent more Twitter followers). I could never know for sure, but I probably had more money in the bank, too!

Yet, our careers had massively different momentum shifts in a short period of time.

Like Tim, my debut book introduced a big new idea. *Return On Influence* was the first book on influence marketing. My book was published and promoted by a huge New York City publisher, McGraw-Hill.

*ROI* didn't hit the *New York Times* Best Seller List, but it was very successful in the business book genre, hitting number one in several Amazon categories for a few weeks. The book earned me interviews and appearances on CBS News, Bloomberg, and *The Wall Street Journal*, to name a few.

Over the years, I've also had an amazing career as a keynote speaker and consultant, and I'm currently up there with Tim among the top 1 percent of all authors on Amazon.

But that's the end of the comparison.

I'm no Tim Ferriss.

I'm not getting calls from Oprah. I can't even get a return call from my plumber.

This book answers the question, "Why not?"

What made the difference? What greased Tim Ferriss' flywheel against all odds and built a global sensation? Was it pure luck, or is there some lesson about momentum we can learn and apply to our own ideas and businesses?

**Spoiler alert:** *Of course* there's a lesson here, and the answer lies in a somewhat obscure idea called *Cumulative Advantage.*

The Principle of Cumulative Advantage states that once a person gains a small advantage over others in their field, that advantage will compound over time into increasingly larger advantages.

*But not always.*

This book explores the fuel for that turbine of success. What is *that difference* that gives an idea, a person, or a business unstoppable momentum?

Even if you don't see any apparent initial advantage in your own life, I'm convinced you can build life-changing momentum by understanding how others turn small ideas into big successes.

At its essence, marketing today is about answering one single question: **"How can we be heard?"** How can we rise above the din of infinite options to create sustainable meaning with an audience or group of customers?

I'm convinced that following the old rules of digital engagement is not enough ... not nearly enough. A content strategy isn't enough. Social media isn't enough. SEO isn't enough. Being great at what you do probably isn't enough.

This book will demonstrate how the world is stacked against us in big ways and small and provide new ideas to help us rise above these barricades.

I can't promise you superstardom—and you probably don't need superstardom—but I'll show you how to build relentless momentum for your idea, your business, and your career even when the odds are stacked against you.

To begin our journey, let's start digging into this rather obscure but fascinating idea of Cumulative Advantage ... and in some cases, Cumulative Disadvantage.

# CHAPTER 1

# THE PORCELLIAN CLUB

Have you seen the movie *The Social Network*?

I thought the most fascinating characters in that film were the Winklevoss brothers—chiseled, wealthy, painfully blond, 6-foot-5, identical-twin, Olympic-level rowers who were cheated out of their stake in Facebook by Mark Zuckerberg.

The reason I liked these fellas so much isn't necessarily because of what happened in the movie. Honestly, they came across as whiney and pompous. It's the real-life story of what happened to them *before* and *after* the movie that makes their story so intriguing.

Tyler and Cameron Winklevoss were born in Southampton, NY, a deeply monied area known as "The Hamptons" and one of the most exclusive enclaves in America. Their father, an academic and entrepreneur, had propelled himself upward from a family of hardworking German immigrant coal miners. He started a consulting firm and an early tech company that helped him become a self-made millionaire.

With their wealth and Hamptons status, the twins were accepted into Brunswick School, an exclusive preparatory academy in Greenwich, CT, where they also started their successful athletic careers as rowers.

The momentum of these early advantages propelled the twins to Harvard University and their fateful connection to Mark Zuckerberg. That's the part in the movie. But what you don't know is that their pedigree also allowed them to get "tapped" into Harvard's most secretive and elite men's fraternity, The Porcellian Club.

Perhaps you have fond memories of your own college sorority, fraternity, or social club. But I suspect none of you have been in an organization like this.

Founded in 1791, the all-male Porcellian Club is the oldest continuously operating social club in America. Blue bloods mostly (although that's been changing in recent years), it was reliably reported that President Franklin D. Roosevelt's greatest disappointment in life was that he never was "tapped" for the Porcellian.[1]

Like being a priest or a mafioso, becoming a Porc brother transcends most other earthly loyalties. One member said that his bond to the old club was so exalted that it could be felt but not analyzed. You're a member for life … and then some. More than one brother is buried at the club site.

While other Ivy League social clubs seek out members based on achievement, The Porcellians seek out candidates with the more elusive qualities of virtue, manliness, and charm. It's less a junior achievers drinking club and more a lifelong circle of powerful and devoted friends.

The club's membership has done pretty well. Among the ranks of former members are President Theodore Roosevelt, several Supreme Court Justices, dozens of military leaders, notable titans of industry, and a few past Harvard presidents.

In other words, this "circle of friends" provides a lifetime of instant access to the upper reaches of business, politics, and society in America.

All of the club's quirkiness and secrets and chants and oaths are aimed at one goal: Cementing lifelong relationships with powerful people, generation to generation. The club's motto is, *The same yesterday, today, and forever.* That pretty much says it all.

Why am I spending so much time describing this club?

Here's a story from a historian of Boston's Trinity Church, H. H. Richardson's architectural masterpiece:

> "In speculating as to why Richardson was chosen as the architect, the 34-year-old possessed one great advantage over the other candidates: as a popular Harvard undergraduate he had been a member of the prestigious Porcellian; thus he needed no introduction to the rector or five of the eleven-man building committee—they were all fellow Porcellian members."[2]

As Porcs, the Winklevoss twins were entitled to a lifetime of special advantage … on top of an already impressive lifetime of special advantage.

## LIFE AFTER FACEBOOK

In 2004, the brothers sued Mark Zuckerberg, claiming that he stole their social networking idea and the early snippets of computer code that eventually became Facebook. The lawsuit dragged on for four years.

During this period the brothers were unemployed, traveling around the world training and competing in rowing events to qualify for the 2008 Summer Olympics in Beijing (they finished sixth). But somehow, even as amateur athletes, they had the resources to maintain a *four-year lawsuit* against Facebook, now one of the most powerful companies in America.

In a last-ditch meeting with Zuckerberg, the Facebook founder (now a billionaire) settled out of court for $65 million. Against the advice of their lawyers, the twins took it as $45 million in stock, and that turned out to be one of the best decisions they ever made. Six years after the IPO, the share price had quintupled, and the twins' holdings were estimated at $500 million.

With their rowing career over, the twins planned to slip back into the tech world, using the settlement money to invest in Silicon Valley startups. But they soon discovered that Zuckerberg's shadow made this impossible. Every company in the Valley had the same endgame: sell their startup to Facebook. Nobody wanted to risk having the last name of the two people Zuckerberg hated most in the world on their spreadsheets.

Despondent, the brothers headed to Ibiza to lick their wounds.

Ibiza is part of a tropical archipelago of Spain in the Mediterranean Sea, well-known for its pristine beaches and trendy clubbing scene.

When I feel blue, I head out for a bike ride. The Winklevoss twins go to Ibiza. Noted.

And there, at the Blue Marlin, a famous beach disco brimming with bronzed, beautiful people, a random encounter changed everything for the twins. They met a man named David Azar, who told them about something called Bitcoin cryptocurrency.

At first, they thought Bitcoin was a scam. But the deeper they delved into the theories behind it, the more they believed it was not only real but significant.

Once they were convinced that Bitcoin actually worked, they made an incredible bet, using part of the Facebook settlement money to buy 120,000 coins, one percent of the entire finite supply at the time.

In an unlikely second act, Tyler and Cameron Winklevoss became the world's first Bitcoin billionaires.

And in perhaps the sweetest revenge story the business world has ever known, Mark Zuckerberg called his old blood rivals for advice as Facebook was launching its own cryptocurrency platform.[3]

You can see that the Winklevoss fortune came from advantages built on advantages. Prep school. Harvard. Porcellians. Facebook windfall. Ibiza. Bitcoin. A billion dollars. It almost seems inevitable.

This is an extreme example of Cumulative Advantage, but it's a useful one because for part of the world, this is how day-to-day life works. I did not grow up in that world, and you probably didn't either. So we need to work the system another way.

## HUMBLE BEGINNINGS

Our exploration of the inner workings of Cumulative Advantage starts in 1968 with a Columbia University professor named Meyer Robert Schkolnick.

Meyer was born into a poor family of Russian Jews who had immigrated to the slums of South Philadelphia in 1904. "We were living the lives of those who would come to be known as the deserving poor," he later wrote, "fueled with the unquestioned premise that things would somehow get better, surely so for the children."

The immigrant family had trouble making ends meet in their new homeland, and a bad situation turned into catastrophe when his father's uninsured dairy shop burned to the ground. Meyer had to go to work as an hourly laborer at an early age to help his struggling family.

But despite his off-and-on schooling, Meyer became a serious scholar. By the age of five, he was walking by himself to the nearby Carnegie Public Library, immersing himself in books on science, history, and especially biographies. He was such a frequent visitor that the librarians adopted him as family.

As an adult, he later remembered that through this library, the "seemingly deprived South Philadelphia slum was providing a youngster with every sort of capital—social capital, cultural capital, human capital … everything except financial capital."

Inspired by a neighbor boy, young Meyer also had dreams of performing as a magician and chose the stage name "Merlin," eventually settling on the less-obvious "Merton" in order to "Americanize" his immigrant-family surname. He was known as Robert King Merton, which he kept as his legal name upon receiving a scholarship to Temple University and later Harvard.

Robert K. Merton eventually became known as the father of modern sociology, coining familiar terms such as "role model," "self-fulfilling prophecy," and "unintended consequences." He is among the most famous sociologists who ever lived, but you've never heard of him because—let's be honest—who can name any famous sociologist?

Merton never forgot his immigrant roots or his lifelong fight for acceptance that eventually influenced an idea he called *The Matthew Effect*.

# THE RICH GET RICHER

As a researcher and university professor, Merton was keenly aware of the exciting ideas percolating all around him. As far back as the 1940s he noticed a paper about the "social stratification in science."[4] Some of his university students were working on their research and protested that the older, more established scholars received disproportionate credit for *the students'* hard work.

Merton was curious. He had witnessed the same handicap throughout his life. The people at the top seemed to have so many built-in advantages that the working-class families could never catch up. The rich just kept getting richer. Advantage produced more advantage.

The professor theorized that a chronic and unfair imbalance existed in the academic world.

But was there a way to prove it?

# THE MATTHEW EFFECT

The professor launched an in-depth analysis of the merits of scientists who had won the ultimate accolade: The Nobel Prize.

His research assistant (who later became his wife) Harriet Zuckerman conducted lengthy interviews with Nobel Laureates.[5]

The Nobel Prize is supposed to be the mark of the world's greatest intellects, but Zuckerman's research found this was not necessarily true. Most winners had made only average contributions to their field, while many scientists who would never receive the prize had contributed much more to the advancement of scientific discovery.[6]

Any person who becomes a Nobel Laureate will be awarded a lifetime of access to the best facilities, the most skilled assistants, and every possible advantage to establish their worth on an even greater scale. The scientific establishment unintentionally creates a class structure by giving the most recognized "celebrities" more chances to succeed and further enhance their status.

Merton documented his assistant's findings in a famous article called "The Matthew Effect in Science: The Reward and Communication Systems of Science are Considered."[7]

"Matthew" in this title refers to a famous verse from the Gospel of Matthew (13:12): "For to the one who has, more will be given, and he will have an abundance, but from the one who has not, even what he has will be taken away."[8]

Put in less stately language, *the rich get richer and the poor get poorer.*

This is not just an idle lament from an ancient text. Merton and Zuckerman showed that Matthew was right.

Over the years, social scientists have proven that the Matthew Effect isn't confined to the academic world. It amplifies inequalities in economic, political, educational, cultural, and social status.[9]

Since Merton's original paper debuted more than 50 years ago, the Matthew Effect is also more commonly referred to as *Cumulative Advantage.*[10]

The most accepted description of this idea is that **the advantage of one individual or group over another grows over time, which means that the inequality of this advantage grows, too.**

Cumulative Advantage magnifies small differences over time and makes it difficult for somebody who is behind to catch up.

- Research shows that those who start with an initial advantage attain better career positions, wealth, social status,[11] educational opportunities, and even health.[12]
- The Matthew Effect has been connected to those receiving Oscar nominations.[13]
- A research study of 20,000 athletes across four sports leagues concluded that those who had the initial advantage of early coaching as children had longer and more profitable professional careers.[14]

# A SIMPLE EXAMPLE

Here's an example of Cumulative Advantage commonly provided in the research:

Suppose that two people have otherwise equal merit, but one starts life with $1,000 in the bank and the other starts with $10,000 in the bank. With a 5 percent interest rate that compounds every year, in year 1, the first account would earn $50 and the second account would earn $500.

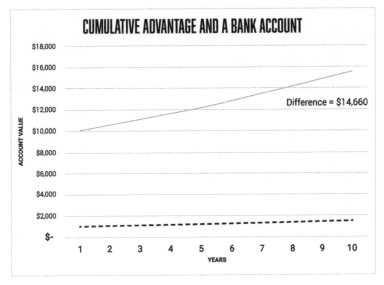

In the first year, the difference in these accounts is $9,450, but after 10 years, the difference would be nearly $15,000. In 20 years, the gap would grow to almost $24,000 … and so on, forever. The broken line at bottom, representing the smaller account, is even hard to pick out as a trendline!

Now imagine that in the first year the starting bank account of the wealthier person had $100,000, or even a cool million. The inequality would compound even more rapidly.

Perhaps a person with that kind of an advantage could afford a private Connecticut prep school, an education at Harvard, dues for a secretive social club, the best lawyers in a lawsuit, and trips to Ibiza to hobnob with influential investors.

You can see that the person with the disadvantage will always be hopelessly behind unless they get a strategic momentum boost somewhere along the line.

The initial advantage that fuels this turbine of momentum doesn't have to be money. It can be unique access to resources, support of influential friends, or being assigned to an advanced academic track in school.

Cumulative Advantage came to Microsoft founder Bill Gates simply because he was one of the only teenagers in the country at the time who had access to early computer prototypes. This allowed him to master coding skills before almost anyone else in his generation.

Dr. Ben Carson, an acclaimed brain surgeon and former U.S. presidential candidate, grew up amid horrific crime and poverty. His illiterate mother expected Ben and his brother to recite a book report to her every week, and the habit kindled an insatiable appetite for reading. Research shows that early acquisition of reading skills leads to a significant long-term academic advantage, while failing to learn to read before the third or fourth grade can result in lifelong learning problems.[15]

If you could somehow plot the Gates "access-to-computers advantage" or the Carson "reading-hundreds-of-books advantage" on a chart like the bank account example above, you would probably see the same widening gap between these leaders and their peers.

Sociologists have been able to reliably record these inequalities so often that they've developed mathematical models to calculate how small advantages grow into big advantages over time. One of these calculations looks like this:

$$
\begin{aligned}
Y_{it} - Y_{it-1} &= \alpha(\delta Y_{i,t-1} + \omega_{it}) + \beta' X_{it} + \upsilon_{it} \\
&= \alpha \delta Y_{i,t-1} + \beta' X_{it} + \alpha \omega_{it} + \upsilon_{it} \\
&= \gamma Y_{i,t-1} + \beta' X_{it} + \varepsilon_{it}.
\end{aligned}
$$

You'll be grateful to know that the only reason I included this formula is to appear geek chic, although there is no proven Matthew Effect advantage to that whatsoever.

Malcolm Gladwell brings the Matthew Effect to popular attention in his book *Outliers*, which I warmly recommend. Gladwell blows apart the fanciful notion of rags-to-riches success:[16]

> "People don't rise from nothing. We do owe something to parentage and patronage. The people who stand before kings may look like they did it all by themselves. But in fact, they are invariably the beneficiaries of hidden advantages and extraordinary opportunities and cultural legacies that allow them to learn and work hard and make sense of the world in ways others cannot.
>
> "It makes a difference where and when we grew up. The culture we belong to and the legacies passed down by our forebears shape the patterns of our achievement in ways we cannot begin to imagine. It's not enough to ask what successful people are like, in other words. It's only by asking where they are from that we can unravel the logic behind who succeeds and who doesn't."

## SOCIAL IMPLICATIONS

By now, you might be thinking that the Matthew Effect could be connected to the convulsions of civil unrest occurring throughout the world. Perhaps you suspect that this idea has very broad social implications.

It does.

Advantage that comes from societal position is a root cause of much of the economic and civil disparity in the world today. In America, some societal advantage can be generated just from being born into the combination of white, male, straight, and able-bodied, to name just a few unearned traits.

The Matthew Effect can either propel ideas forward or breed injustice, resentment, and an invisible caste system that holds worthy people back from success.

I need to interrupt our regular programming to explain a decision I made regarding the scope of this book. You could write a massive volume based on that last paragraph alone, and I hope somebody will do it. But I'm not the right person to carry that torch. I leave this vast and important opportunity to passionate authors far more qualified than me, although I will humbly add a personal perspective on this at the end of this book.

Here's what interests me … and I hope it interests you. We know that Cumulative Advantage exists everywhere in business and society. It's either working for us or against us. So is there a way *anybody* can systematically put Cumulative Advantage to productive use and be more successful?

In Robert Merton's original description of Cumulative Advantage, he taunts us with a tantalizing clue. He said the gap between haves and have-nots will always grow unless there are *countervailing processes*.

He suggests that we can unwind this forever pattern by identifying these countervailing processes and applying them to our own lives, careers, and businesses. But he doesn't explicitly tell us what they are!

I've spent the last two years trying to figure that out—and share it with you in this book.

# FOUNDATIONS OF ADVANTAGE

Let's return to Mr. Unlikely-Success-Machine Tim Ferriss and re-examine his case study. How did the momentum of Cumulative Advantage work for him?

Tim was brilliant and ambitious, but he was no entitled Winklevoss. He needed to develop some **initial advantage** on his own to get his turbine moving, and indeed, it was a relatively small one: an idea for a unique approach to working less and enjoying life more. Most publishers hated it, but against all odds, it was the catalyst for his colossal success.

Next, Tim attributes much of his success to timing. He published his book at the beginning of the irrational "hustle" lifestyle that was burning people out and snuffing out dreams and relationships. A four-hour workweek? Sign me up! But how did Tim know the moment is right for his idea? Once he validated a **seam of opportunity**, he burst through it with full force.

Tim helped assure his success by creating a relentless "**sonic boom**" **of promotion** for his idea. He cultivated relationships with powerful bloggers who were eager to promote his ideas when the book came out.

**Powerful friends provided him with insight and access.** Once the turbine started to wind up, he leveraged his early success into powerful new mentoring relationships that taught him how to invest and evaluate promising startups. Having these new friends provided credibility, admission to Oprah Orbit, and connections with even more power, knowledge, and resources.

Finally, Tim had **constancy of purpose**. He didn't stop with one idea or one book. Tim made a series of good decisions that kept the momentum going. After the success of *The 4-Hour Workweek*, he made a career of teaching fans how to achieve personal goals using the least amount of time and effort, and he did that through his franchise of books, speeches, and workshops.

The book-long "momentum competition" between myself and Tim Ferriss is meant to be a whimsical and entertaining device to teach a serious lesson. The five factors that led to Tim's momentum were also documented in original research I sponsored through Samantha Stone and the Marketing Advisory Network.[17] We wanted to discern which factors help entrepreneurs build enough momentum for an idea so that it becomes a profitable business.

Of course these factors are not limited to the business world. Knowing how to build momentum can help support any idea: a social cause, a political platform, an artistic movement. But we found that this survey group was easy to identify and easy to measure: Were they successful or not? How did they get there?

When we asked business founders for the biggest contributors to their momentum, they responded this way:

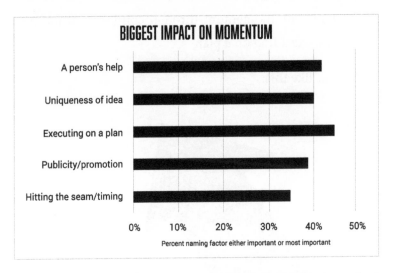

**BIGGEST IMPACT ON MOMENTUM**

Percent naming factor either important or most important

You can see that these five factors are fairly tightly packed in terms of importance. To learn more about this research and to find other helpful free resources to support your own path to Cumulative Advantage, please visit the dedicated book website at *www.businessesGROW/CumulativeAdvantage.*

The formula from the Ferriss case study and my research is the recipe we'll follow for the rest of the book. If we aren't born into Cumulative Advantage, we can go around the system and make it work for us another way when we:

1. Identify an initial advantage

2. Discover a seam of timely opportunity

3. Create significant awareness for our project through a "sonic boom" of promotion

4. Gain access to a higher orbit by reaching out and reaching up to powerful allies

5. Build the momentum through constancy of purpose and executing on a plan

It looks like this:

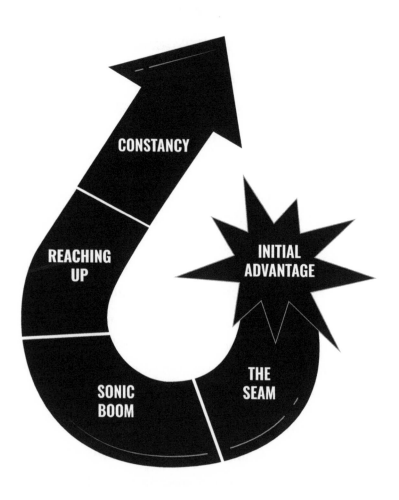

Let's begin our quest for Cumulative Advantage. How do we find that one small advantage that sets our success momentum in motion?

The answer comes from an unexpected place: Everywhere.

# INITIAL ADVANTAGE

*"If I can master the negative forces and harness them to my chariot, they can work to my advantage."*

—INGMAR BERGMAN

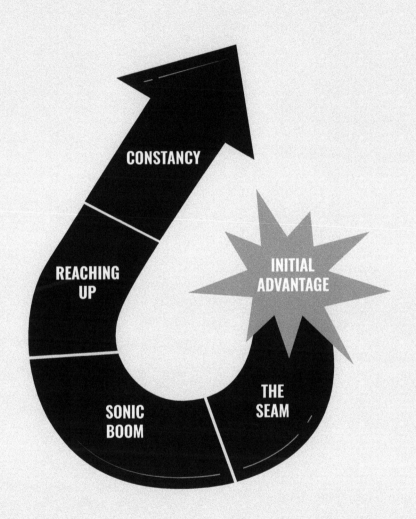

# CHAPTER 2

# ONE SMALL SPARK

At the height of my corporate marketing career, I was asked to lead my company's first eCommerce team.

Some thought this move was a career death sentence. I had been heading up the global marketing efforts for the most important business unit in the company. Why would I take a chance on something unknown … like the internet?

But it wasn't unknown to me!

In the earliest days of the web, I said to my boss, "You know, I think there's something to this internet thing. I'd like to get a company AOL subscription and put it on my expense account."

After a short deliberation, my request was approved, and I was the first person in this Fortune 100 corporation to have a company-approved internet subscription. I was no Bill Gates, but I did gain an instant advantage over my peers!

As I learned more about the World Wide Web, I began to develop valuable new processes to help my company buy and sell scrap metal online—one of the earliest B2B marketplaces anywhere—and the idea actually worked.

A few years later, my company finally woke up and was ready to make a multi-million-dollar investment in an eCommerce strategy (whatever that meant). They needed a leader for this daring new venture, and I was just about the only marketing executive in the company who had any internet experience, courtesy of my expensed AOL account.

My first "internet job" would be to lead a global business powerhouse into the digital age at a time when most company leaders could barely turn on a computer. I was expecting massive resistance to change, starting with my boss, who refused to adopt email.

I had no corporate mandate. The company was made up of 45 independent business units. To be successful, I would have to convince each business president why my team should exist and be funded.

I didn't know it at the time, but my little department's momentum wasn't built on an idea, strategy, or budget windfall. It turned out to be this: We were first, and we were cool.

With my initial budget funding, I effectively created an internet startup within the company to develop and commercialize a custom eCommerce platform across all business units. This was the bleeding edge of business at the time, and many of the brightest people in the company wanted to be part of my team. To put this in perspective, my project launched in 2001 ... three years before Facebook started. So yes, we were far ahead of our time. And that was cool.

As my eCommerce vision was coded into existence, my strategy included small and measurable victories that I promoted like crazy so people could begin to understand what we were doing.

As our success gained momentum, I didn't have to pitch my ideas to the business units anymore. They began coming to me because they wanted to be cool, too. Here's what our online revenue growth looked like:

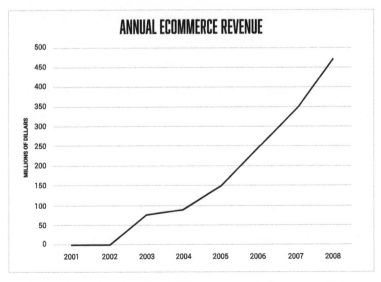

When the momentum ramped up, I attracted more people, more resources, and more attention.

Arguably, the *initial advantage* I had created by selling my boss on that dial-up connection propelled me into this promotion, which propelled me to the leading edge of eCommerce, which propelled me into digital marketing consulting, teaching, speaking, and writing ... where I am today.

Advantage led to advantage.

## THE RACE CONTINUES

Let's return to the Ferriss-Schaefer Paths of Momentum.

I just revealed that I would not be writing this book today if I had not asked my boss to pay for an AOL internet account. That initial advantage helped me gain precious experience and career momentum.

My life today as a speaker, author, and digital marketing consultant was not the result of a grand vision or plan—my career tumbled forward out of that small first spark. The thought of writing a book never crossed my mind until I was nearly 50 years old. I didn't give my first paid speech until I was 51.

But you can trace all this success back to one moment when I sheepishly asked my boss if it was OK to be on the internet while I was at work—a revolutionary idea at the time!

What about Tim Ferriss? What was the inspiration for him to become a self-help guru?

He lost his girl.

After college, Tim started a nutritional supplement

company and nearly worked himself to death. One of the casualties of his never-stop-hustling lifestyle was a long-term romantic relationship.

On the edge of psychological and physical self-destruction, Tim sold his company and spent years trying to figure out what went wrong. Something had to change. He began a process of "extricating himself from a self-made prison of a startup."[1]

Tim traveled the world, obsessed about discovering, testing, and refining any life hacks that would give him more peace and joy in life.

And those hacks became the idea behind his book. So, in a weird way, his girlfriend ending their relationship set into motion a chain of events that led Tim to where he is today.

This is beginning to sound more than a little strange. For both of us, the monumental turning point of our careers emerged from ... *normal life events*.

We weren't "following a dream." There was no plan, no strategy, not even an a-ha moment. The catalyst that created momentum and a path toward Cumulative Advantage was a weird and random event.

Turns out, it almost *always* works this way.

## SUCCESS IS A COLLISION OF EVENTS

Researcher Frans Johansson codified this mysterious idea that every success starts with a "click moment"—a collision of people and ideas and circumstances that creates your one small advantage.[2]

I like to think that this is what happened to Bruce Wayne when he discovered the Bat Cave. "Oh my gosh. The perfect lair! And it was right under my home all this time."

According to Johansson, nearly every great breakthrough starts with one of these moments.

For instance, in 1963, the American radiologist Charles Dotter accidentally threaded a catheter through a clogged artery during a diagnostic procedure. To his surprise, he found that the accident ended up helping his patient.

A couple of years later another physician learned of Dotter's breakthrough at a lecture in Germany. Suddenly he made a connection and realized that he could take this treatment even further by using inflatable balloons small enough to pass into tiny coronary arteries.

Thus, angioplasty surgery was born from a mistake. The regularity with which chance discoveries are made in science has led some historians to describe serendipity as a significant factor in the evolution of science.[3]

I love the cinematic spectacle of the Marvel Universe movies. But I'd never be able to cheer for Iron Man if a 15-year-old boy named Stanley Lieber hadn't won a newspaper essay contest in 1937. When he won the contest three times in a row, the newspaper editor encouraged him to become a professional writer.

As a teenager, the only writing job he could find was with a new publishing company called Timely Comics. When the company's creative team suddenly quit, the desperate owner elevated the 19-year-old Lieber to editor.

Lieber was so embarrassed to be working for a comic book company that he insisted on being called "Stan Lee" to hide his true identity.

Lee went on to become a publishing icon and the creator of Spider-Man, Black Panther, the X-Men, and an entire universe of other characters. Spider-Man and Batman in the same chapter of my book? Huzzah!

Kristian Bush is one of Nashville's most prolific singer-songwriters and is best known for being one half of the Grammy-winning, multi-platinum band Sugarland. Kristian told me that a mashup of early life events created an initial advantage that propelled him into music business momentum:

- As children, he and his brother were among the very first students enrolled in pilot classes for the Suzuki method music training programs.

- Inexpensive four-track cassette recording technology became available that allowed him to teach himself how to produce a record.

- As a teenager, his mom bought him access to a professional music studio as a birthday present.

"By the time I'm 15 or 16 years old, I knew the entire mechanics of a record company," he said. "I knew how much time it takes to record, how much money it takes, what the physical effort is, and then what the payoff is for each choice that I made.

"Because of these weird events, I'm walking into high school with the complete ability to make a band and make a record. Since this was the only thing I had going for me in terms of a chance to get a girlfriend, I kept it going. I knew I could get to you through your headphones.

"This accumulated knowledge was unique, and it gave me a huge advantage when I got my first contract on a major label. I had fundamental knowledge that my peers didn't even have anything close to."

So much seems to rely on chance, doesn't it? Recall that even the Winklevoss twins were led to a billion-dollar fortune through a random meeting with a stranger in a bar on the beach.

For fun (really), I sent out a questionnaire to 25 of my most successful and powerful friends with a simple question: "Did your success come from a plan or strategy, or did it come from a random event?"

Frans Johansson was right. Every single person told me the initial spark for their career success was ignited by a random event.

## A SECRET WORLD OF SUCCESS

If so much of an idea's success is due to chance, why don't we hear about it? Why is this such a well-kept secret?

Turns out, there's a very good reason.

Chilean sociologists Mario Molina and Mauricio Bucca noticed that when their friends played a card game that was totally based on chance, they insisted that their winning streak was based on superior skills. This inspired Molina and Bucca to do experiments that helped them discover that same fascinating pattern repeating over and over—if a person has success, they are almost entirely unable to separate their role from the role played by sheer luck.[4]

"Luck is not something you can mention in the presence of self-made men," E.B. White wrote many years ago.

In this entrepreneurial economy, there are more and more self-made men and women, and they are becoming increasingly convinced of their own success, even when they've had a lot of luck and help along the way, according to economist Robert H. Frank and other researchers.[5]

Of course hard work is necessary for success. If we're biking into the wind, we'll feel the difference right away. We have to pedal harder, we're sweating, and we're getting tired.

But if we have tailwind, it feels different. After a while, we don't even notice its assistance anymore. We can easily picture people heading into a strong wind, but it's far more difficult to capture an image of the wind at our backs. It's almost as if it were invisible.

In short, we tend to forget the luck that is the wind at our backs, but we never forget the headwind and the hard work. And that becomes our public narrative.

Most initial advantage is based on chance—where we were born, who we met, a lucky break along the way—but we never explain it that way!

That's troubling, because a growing body of evidence from Frank[6] and others suggests that seeing ourselves as self-made—rather than as talented, hardworking, *and* lucky—leads us to be less generous and public-spirited. It may even make the lucky ones less likely to support the conditions that made their own success possible (like high-quality public infrastructure and education).

Psychologists use the term *hindsight bias* to describe our tendency to think, after the fact, that an event was predictable … even when it wasn't. This bias operates with particular force for unusually successful people.

# CLICK MOMENTS AND THE CORPORATION

The random sparks that propel individual momentum also create new organizations and companies.

Take the example of Nike. Bill Bowerman, a legendary running coach, was having breakfast one morning with his wife while they discussed a thorny challenge: how to develop a spikeless sports shoe.

Then he saw his wife pry a waffle from their waffle iron. It was a fateful moment as Bowerman, without saying a word, sprinted back to his lab and returned with two cans of chemicals which, when mixed, created latex. He poured them into the waffle iron. Could the small "spikes" on a waffle grip the running track without damaging it and still provide comfort to the runner?

He poured three more latex waffles and combined them into one shoe. The answer was yes. The experiment worked. That random moment represented a turning point for the shoe company and launched a global athletic apparel empire.

Sara Blakely founded her company Spanx after staring at her closet in frustration one day. She explained:[7]

"Like many women, I had all these great clothes hanging in my closet, unworn, because I couldn't figure out what to wear *under* it. The options were not that great. I spent all my hard-earned money on this one pair of cream pants that hung there, and I decided to cut the feet out of control-top pantyhose one day, and I threw them on under my white pants and went to a party. I looked fabulous, I felt great, I had no panty lines, I looked thinner and smoother, but they rolled up my legs all night. And I remember thinking, 'This product should exist for women.'

"I'd never taken a business class. I'd never worked in fashion or retail. I'd been selling fax machines door-to-door for seven years, and I had $5,000 in savings. I'd just moved out of my mom's house, and I was dating a loser. So, my life was great.

"I went on the internet and found that the bulk of hosiery in the United States is made in North Carolina. I started calling all of these hosiery mills and said, 'Please help me make this idea of this footless, pantyhose-shaper concept.' Everybody hung up on me, and I tried that for several months with no luck.

"The problem was, I was explaining to men how I was going to change the world for women. They couldn't understand the concept. Since no one's talking to me on the phone, I took a week off of work and drove around North Carolina in person, trying to convince somebody to help make my product. After cold-calling these mills for a week, I went back to Atlanta with no luck.

"Two weeks later, I got a phone call from one of the mill owners, and he said, 'Sara, I've decided to help make your crazy idea.' When I asked him why he had a change of heart, he simply said, 'I have two daughters.'

"He had run my idea by his daughters, and they said, 'Dad, this idea is actually brilliant, and makes sense. You should help her do it.' And that set me on a journey to make the first prototype."

Today, Spanx is a billion-dollar enterprise.

Business consultant Martin Lindstrom estimates that 84 percent of all businesses started from a random event.[8] Fortune 500 companies like Starbucks and Home Depot and products such as Velcro, Viagra, Band-Aids, and Post-It Notes emerged from a single customer insight or a serendipitous event. Anita Roddick, a human rights activist and environmental campaigner, founded The Body Shop as a response to one customer's request for ethical consumerism.

We love reading these inspiring founder stories but probably don't consider how random connections are *happening to us all the time* … and how they could propel our own momentum.

# RANDOMNESS IN ACTION

In this book's introduction, I mention that, like Tim Ferriss, my first book was a turning point in my life. The click moment for the *Return On Influence* book came when I met another entrepreneur at a conference.

In 2009, a controversial startup called Klout burst onto the scene. Founder Joe Fernandez audaciously claimed that by applying complex algorithms to analyze patterns of social media content, he could predict how influential you are.

The internet howled with indignation! Who would have the arrogance to assign a number (from 0-100) that reflected a person's relative power rating on the web?

Today of course, we take these influence algorithms for granted. There are dozens of companies offering influencer marketing services, and they all use a model based on what Klout started.

But at the time, Joe and his little company took a relentless beating from critics. I have never seen a hard-working company founder attacked so viciously.

But I was starting to think Klout might be on to something.

In those early days, Justin Bieber was the only person who had a perfect "100" Klout score (he was one point higher than President Barack Obama). The company explained that the Bieber fans reacted to whatever the teen heartthrob said on social media. If The Biebs said, "Go see this movie," his fans went to the movie.

If you could actually track behaviors and connect them to a person's tweet or Facebook post … well, isn't that influence?[9]

The click moment that changed my life came at the annual SXSW conference, my favorite gathering of global thought leaders. Since Klout was generating so much buzz, Joe Fernandez had been invited to speak there.

His panel presentation was predictably filled with fireworks from the standing-room-only ballroom crowd, but Joe was calm and patient. A mob gathered around him afterwards, and I hung around until the end, hoping to snag a conversation with the Klout founder.

When I met him, Joe was friendly and willing to be interviewed for my blog. As he explained how his algorithm worked, I had an epiphany.

People were upset with Klout because they claimed their influence in the "real world" had no connection to their posts on the web. But in a flash of inspiration I realized that influence on the web *only came from one thing*—the ability to move content!

Fernandez was right. He *could* measure influence. But not everywhere, and not for everybody. He could track the people on the web who could most efficiently spread ideas—and that was a revolutionary concept for business and marketers. Joe was identifying the new tastemakers, the cool kids, the rising stars ready to make a dent in the universe through their blogs and videos and tweets.

The idea for my book lit up before me like an airport runway. I knew the marketing world was about to be transformed.

We were being handed an entirely new way to connect to consumers—through these trusted influencers and their fans … and I knew this would happen quickly.

The world had been dominated by elite power brokers—TV network executives, ad industry big shots, and publishing companies. But once we could actually identify these new "citizen influencers," the power would shift and we'd enter an era of "influencer marketing," a term nobody was using yet.

New York publisher McGraw-Hill took a risk on the book idea, for which I will forever be grateful because *Return On Influence* thrust me onto the national stage.

I never had a plan to write books for a living. Everything unfolded from that one conversation in an Austin, Texas, hotel ballroom.

Most people think they're lucky to have a meaningful insight like that once in their lives, but the fact is, these click moments are happening constantly … they're probably just not registering

We'd like to believe that exceptional strategy, planning, and leadership are the drivers of success because that's what is taught in school. All of those things are definitely important. But the truth is, success is far more random than we believe.

I hope you consider this to be exciting and encouraging news. You don't have to be Einstein—or even Tim Ferriss—to find your own groundbreaking ideas. You just have to put yourself in a place to have experiences that give you a chance.

In the next chapter, we'll find out exactly how to do that.

# CHAPTER 3

# ACTING ON CURIOSITY

Ragy Thomas is the founder and CEO of a fast-growing, billion-dollar tech company ... and it all started because he was an email geek.

His company, Sprinklr, provides software that enables large organizations to listen to, engage, and reach customers across social channels to deliver better customer experiences. But the first spark for his big idea came by noticing patterns between emerging social media platforms and the problems he had already solved for email marketing customers.

Before the emergence of social media, email was the most efficient way to connect the world, and Ragy had built one of the first email software companies. "To build an email marketing platform," he said, "I had to invent different pieces: content planning, publishing, approval workflows, automation, governance. All the different capabilities enterprises needed to use for email marketing, I built.

"When social media started to get big, my 'aha moment' came when I realized that marketers would have to solve the same problems that I had already solved at scale with email.

"If you look at LinkedIn or Facebook or Twitter—they all had private direct message features similar to email, and they all had a news feed. If I became a friend or started following you, you're giving me permission to connect with you … just like email. I realized the main problems I solved with email marketing could be applied to these new social media channels. It crystallized what I wanted to do."

Ragy started Sprinklr in a spare bedroom in 2009 and earned his first customer one year later. By following his curiosity about social media content patterns and matching them to customer needs, he was able to continuously grow his platform.

"The second aha moment," he said, "was when I realized that for the first time, the billions of people connected on social media aren't fragmented, individual strands. There are patterns to these connections that could be grouped and codified. I knew that would deeply disrupt marketing and advertising as we knew it. This would change customer care forever because now people can instantly create a one-star review that can influence thousands of people. No company can afford to let that happen.

"The third aha came with artificial intelligence. By applying AI to an enormous number of social media conversations, we could identify elusive needles in the haystack—customer insights that allowed us to know with precision what we should be doing with our business."

Just 10 years after Ragy started coding in his spare bedroom, Sprinklr counts mega-brands like Nike, McDonald's, and Samsung among its customers.

The beginning of this successful company came from the fact that Ragy Thomas was curious and continuously *acted on that curiosity*. By noticing something new and exploring an idea, a tiny, unexpected spark was fanned into a flame of creative energy. As I explain in Chapter 2, this initial advantage sets the momentum of Cumulative Advantage into motion.

# THE ENERGETIC QUEST

Maybe you're thinking these random moments are pure luck, a mystical force beyond your control—unless you're a Jedi master. But there are specific actions you can take to sway serendipitous fate in your favor.

Systematic innovation is made possible by being aware of the ideas bombarding you every day, thinking about how these ideas might solve a current problem or connect to your life experiences, and then taking action.

One researcher wrote, "While good luck may befall the inert or lazy, serendipitous discovery occurs only in the course of an *energetic quest*—a quest in which lucky discoveries can be recognized through alertness and then exploited."[1]

For example, the catalytic flash for my first book seemed lucky, but it was actually the result of an "energetic quest." I had an idea about the nature of online influence and how it might change marketing forever. I followed my curiosity and had the conversation with Joe Fernandez. When I waited 30 minutes in line to talk to the Klout founder, I nudged fate my way, which is something anyone can do. And the more times you nudge fate, the better your chances at ultimate success.

Most important, once I made the connection between an ability to move content and online influence, I *acted on the idea*, kicking the momentum into high gear.

Margaret Heffernan, a professor at the University of Bath, said an entrepreneurial leader today has to pursue curiosity like an artist: "What does an artist do? They notice, they investigate, they seek to understand what's really going on in the world. Then they ask themselves this question constantly— 'what can we make of it?' How can we make something that's really positive, that's relevant, that speaks to people, that is meaningful and has value? They have a fearless imagination and endless capacity to experiment. They change before they have to. They keep moving. And they recognize that they often fail."[2]

Tim Ferriss was inspired to write a book as he traversed the world mourning a longtime personal relationship that fell victim to his workaholic lifestyle. That resulted in an insight, and Ferriss acted on the idea with determination, doggedly pursuing a book deal even after 26 rejections.

Unique insights are random, unexpected, and serendipitous.

Sustainable success requires that we tune in to more of those click moments all around us. The challenge is, how do we set ourselves up for those opportunities?

You just need the recipe.

I once had the opportunity to interview the great writer and historian Walter Isaacson. He has written incredible books on intellectual giants—Steve Jobs, Albert Einstein, Benjamin Franklin—and I asked him about his definition of genius. How did these icons receive their inspiration?

He told me that insight requires two conditions: endless curiosity and the ability to see patterns.

In other words, creating insights comes from being curious and connecting the dots in a new way. You call on your unique life experience to look at something from a different angle.

In an academic paper titled "Serendipity in Entrepreneurship," Nicholas Dew contends that the most important spark of new ideas comes when individuals are involved in some kind of an inquisitive search and accidentally bump into something they weren't looking for.[3]

The beginning of momentum is *acting on curiosity.*

Some new idea grips you, and furious napkin-writing ensues. You forget to eat. You build a prototype. This kernel starts a nuclear chain reaction that fuels a new passion.

Inspiration seldom bowls you over. It's usually a gentle hand on your shoulder guiding you forward toward something new.

You can certainly be intentional about acting on an inspiration that starts the road to Cumulative Advantage.

Here are six ways anybody can become more insight-driven:

## 1. Connect your present to your past

One of my favorite ways of creating insights is applying an experience from the past to a situation in the present.

Here is a universal truth: If you're reading this book, you have a past, and you have a present ... so you should be able to do this!

In my own original research conducted with Samantha Stone and Marketing Advisory Network, I found that 72 percent of successful entrepreneurs started their business based on prior life experiences, without the benefit of any outside research.

The Joe Fernandez story I relate in Chapter 2 is an example of this idea. By the time I had that conversation with Joe, I had been in marketing for more than 25 years. I had been creating content for the social web for four years. It's possible that *nobody else* would have had the same insight from that conversation if they had not had *my* unique history and perspective.

Consider another example, Alberto "Beto" Perez, a dancer from Cali, Colombia.

As a teenager, Beto taught step aerobics in the evenings to pay for his dance lessons. It was boring, but it was good money.

Then his two interests collided. Beto showed up one night to teach an aerobics class and realized he had forgotten his usual music. He searched his backpack and found a mix tape full of salsa and merengue songs. Rather than cancel class, Beto decided to scrap the normal routine and improvise the entire class by integrating his high-energy dance routines. The class loved it!

The intersection of a problem with Beto's past experience created a flash of inspiration, and Zumba was born. There are now Zumba classes in 186 countries, reaching 15 million people (by comparison McDonald's is in just 118 countries!).[4] This rapid success never would have happened if Beto hadn't combined a random circumstance with his life experience. Most important, he responded to the enthusiasm of his class and took action.

Aheda Zanetti, born in Lebanon and raised in Sydney, was watching her niece play netball (the Aussie version of basketball) when she had an epiphany. Her niece's face shone with sweat, and Aheda realized that if she could create an active garment in the mode of Muslim traditional dress, she'd solve her niece's problem. Eventually she came up with the Hijood—a special headgear for athletes seeking to win glory without compromising their faith. Now she has 23 employees and her products are available worldwide

Likewise, Ragy Thomas' flash of inspiration about the nature of social media could have only dawned on him because of his unique background observing patterns in email communication.

Nobody can have an insight exactly like you … because there's only one you. You are an insight machine.

## 2. Connect the people

While I was writing my last book, I read a biography of Leonardo DaVinci, arguably the most creative human being who ever lived.

What struck me was that many of his greatest ideas were collaborative. Even his most famous illustration, "Vitruvian Man"—you know, the naked dude in the circle—was inspired by Vitruvius, a Roman author, architect, and civil engineer who lived centuries before Leonardo's time.

Leonardo was a beloved man—and a bit of a partier—who was always surrounded by friends. One day, his friend Francesco showed him a sketch of a man within a circle based on the detailed descriptions from a Vitruvian book. It spurred Leonardo to consider the dimensions of a human being in mathematical terms.

Another friend, Giacomo Andrea, scribbled some interpretations of the Vitruvian idea and showed Leonardo how the human figure could be circumscribed in a circle.

Leonardo was captivated by the idea and inspired to find his own manuscript of Vitruvius' ancient work. He developed his own drawing from those ideas, and in both scientific precision and artistic beauty, his illustration is in an entirely different realm than the work of his predecessors.

The now-famous drawing was built upon an ancient idea that inspired a scribbled drawing by a friend that led to a discussion with yet another person. Yes, Leonardo delivered something exquisite and unique, but it only could have happened with the help of his friends.

As I read about this, I reflected on my own creative process. Writing my previous books had largely been a lonely and isolated ordeal. Of course, I did research and interviews. But in terms of framing the book, it was all taking place by myself … in a big chair, in a quiet office, in total isolation. I became inspired by Leonardo and set upon a plan to speak to and, in most cases, meet with thought leaders who could help forge the main ideas of the book.

This group of people, who I fondly called my "DaVinci Team," had a profound impact on the beauty and depth of the *Marketing Rebellion* book. It worked so well that I formed a new DaVinci Team for this book, and you can read about them in the Acknowledgments at the end.

Leonardo DaVinci didn't necessarily "think outside of the box." His creative breakthroughs came from mashing up the ideas of other people.

When I was in graduate school studying applied behavioral sciences, I learned that your basic mental framework—how you process information—is essentially complete by the time you're 15 years old. So literally, it's impossible for you to think "outside of the box" because you're permanently hard-wired to think in a certain way.

Creating insights comes through *combining* boxes, or tumbling mental frameworks in new ways.

The greatest proof of this is a creativity technique I learned many years ago called "brain writing." I've used this in consulting sessions with Dell, Microsoft, and other companies to create spark moments with impressive success.

Plan a brainstorming session with at least 10 diverse people. Really shake up the diversity in every way you can. And the more people involved, the better. I've done this technique successfully with as many as 75 people.

Be sure to tell everyone ahead of time what the purpose of the brainstorming meeting is and that they should come prepared with at least a few ideas.

Early in your meeting, have everybody rip off a big piece of easel paper and write their very best idea for the brainstorming topic at the top of the page. Make sure there's plenty of room below their idea to write additional ideas.

Have them hang their papers on the walls around the room and stand in front of them.

Ask everybody to slide over one space to their right so that they're standing in front of the idea next to them. Tell the participants to read the idea written at the top and then add to or improve the original idea, writing their contribution below it.

Next, have everybody slide over TWO spaces—not just one! You don't want the same person continually following the thought process of the person in front of them. You're trying to mix up the mental frameworks—mash up the boxes!

Tell them to write a *better* idea based on what's on the page so far, and then have everybody slide again. This time count off three spaces. Read what has been written so far and add to it or improve it once again.

You can repeat this process another four or five times until every page is full of ideas.

Have each participant go back to their original idea, read the entire page, and circle the best idea.

This is when the magic happens. About 95 percent of the time, the best idea they circle is *not their original idea*! In less than 30 minutes you can turn all of your good ideas into great—perhaps even breakthrough—sparks of innovation.

This idea of "combining boxes" shows why diversity is so important. You don't want to do this exercise when everybody is a numbers-type or creative-type or even all of a certain age or cultural heritage. The more "boxes" you combine, the better the results. Always!

Combining boxes doesn't have to occur on a team. For me, it's an everyday process where I talk to people who are willing to build ideas with me.

One go-to friend for insight-building is Keith Reynold Jennings, an executive with Jackson Healthcare in Atlanta. A few years ago, we were riffing together in a hotel lobby and I asked him what obscure research he knew about that should be applied to business in a new way. "Cumulative Advantage," he replied.

Hmmmmm … not a bad idea!

Actionable insights are so much more likely to come from conversations than from sitting in an office. Get out there and combine some boxes.

## 3. Go where the action is

I spend a lot of time mentoring kids from poorer neighborhoods in my city. One time, I was struggling to get them to do their homework on time—a never-ending battle.

But when I visited them in their home, I had an insight. I realized they had no Wi-Fi in the house! Of course it was hard to do their homework!

I never would have had that realization unless I had been standing in the middle of the situation. They had been too shy to tell me about the problem.

In the same way, I get incredible insights through firsthand observations of my customers and their facilities.

In my corporate days, I was immersed in the Toyota Production System and learned of the Kaizen principle of "going to gemba."

*Gemba* is a Japanese term meaning "the real place." In business, *gemba* refers to the place where value is created. The most common use of the term is in manufacturing, where the *gemba* is usually the factory floor, but it can be anywhere you attain new insight by *seeing*.

It's nearly impossible to understand what others are thinking when you're sitting alone at your desk. Designers and product developers have long understood how important it is to take this anthropological approach.

The master of this technique is consultant and author Martin Lindstrom, who has made a career of this immersive strategy. He told me about a project he led to rebrand a hotel:

"We work with one of the most luxurious hotel chains in the world and they asked us to redefine the concept of 'suites.' The problem is, you can stay at the crappiest hotel and they all call themselves suites, right? So, it's a completely watered-down word, but the suites in five-star hotels might cost $1,000, $2,000, or $10,000 a night. So, it really is a bit of an elastic word that needed to be rebranded.

"We started by interviewing the luxury hotel guests. I literally sat down with 15 billionaires. I learned that people buy these suite experiences because they want to go through a transformation in their lives. It's not just a matter of having the biggest room, or the best bed, or even more amenities in the bathroom. They're so used to all that stuff anyway.

"What they really want is a unique memory to take home with them. That was the key insight!

"These hotels are serious properties that have an enormous amount of history in each and every suite. Problem was, nobody ever recorded those iconic stories—people living or not living, famous songs composed in those rooms, books we all know were written there, amazing movies filmed at the locations. In some cases, a celebrity had lived in one room for more than 20 years! But nobody had connected these stories to the suites.

"We created a history team, and the team went around the world, went into the suites, interviewed past staff, existing staff, customers, guests, anybody who had a story to tell. And we have rebranded all the suites by integrating the history, the celebrities, the stories into every room in a very classy and subtle way.

"The point here is that often brands are sitting on a gold mine of opportunity. We didn't create more value for this company by changing the product or service in any physical way. But we changed it a lot in an *emotional way* by visiting these places and seeing them in a new light."

## 4. Is the dog barking?

One of the great honors of my life was studying under the great American author and consultant Peter Drucker, perhaps the most respected business strategist in history.

He would teach us through the case study method, and you could see him wind up with excitement as his students closed in on solving these complex business entanglements.

One of his favorite phrases was "but the dog isn't barking." He was referencing a story by Sir Arthur Conan Doyle called "The Adventure of Silver Blaze." In this story, his heroic Sherlock Holmes character solved a mystery because a dog that should have been barking at a stranger wasn't barking … so the suspect had to be someone the dog knew.

If you're in a situation where you would expect to hear a dog barking and it's not, never ignore that clue! This is an anomaly that can almost always lead to momentous insight.

Businesses today are awash in data. Innovators pore over this information looking for promising ideas, but they often focus on averages and obvious patterns, which lead to broad conclusions. Most likely, the real insights lie in the results that *deviate* from business as usual.

A few years ago, I had a chance work on a consulting project in Russia. One might think that this vast country with more than 100 million middle-class consumers and 75 million internet subscribers would be an attractive market for online retail.

But e-commerce accounts for a paltry 1.5 percent of total retail sales in the country. That makes no sense! The dog wasn't barking. What was going on here?

As I dug into it, I learned the reasons for the anomaly are that the Russian postal system is terrible and few consumers have credit cards. This incongruity led retailers to develop many new innovations including company-owned delivery systems and private lock boxes for customer pick-up in isolated cities.

When something in your life or business doesn't make sense, dig deeper. There's a spark to be discovered.

## 5. See opportunities in crisis

Every great idea meets some unmet or under-served need. Every crisis reveals an entirely new set of consumer needs that may shift into permanent opportunities.

Early in the coronavirus pandemic, my wife contracted the disease on a family ski trip to Sun Valley, Idaho. A few days after she returned home with a fever, I became ill with the disease, too. Thank you, my dear!

The coronavirus hit us hard. At that time, there were no treatments. The strategy was to let the virus roll through your body and hope you didn't have to go to the hospital.

Combining the amount of time we were either sick or quarantined, we were confined to our home for more than 50 days. Although I had been stockpiling some dry goods before the pandemic hit us, we were unable to obtain any fresh food for nearly two months!

Then I received an email from a local cattle rancher. "I know the local restaurants are closed and you can't enjoy our beef," he wrote. "So we'll bring our steaks to you and drop it off at your door."

What a lifesaver. This entrepreneurial rancher saw opportunity in crisis and acted on it.

Likewise, we started subscribing to HelloFresh, a useful and low-cost service that delivers fresh meat and vegetables to your door along with prescribed recipes. This kept us supplied during our lockdowns, and we discovered that we liked learning new recipes! So even though we're no longer sick, we still use the service today.

Imagine that. My wife and I are buying a portion of our food through a channel we didn't even know existed before our health crisis.

Even the civil unrest in America and other parts of the world can forge new ideas. Attitudes are changing. Expectations of companies and their leaders are shifting. The rules of consumer engagement are being rewritten.[5]

Every downturn and downfall exposes magnificent opportunities for new ideas.

## 6. Create a collision-prone environment

As we learned through the Matthew Effect, some people have a permanent, baked-in advantage that leads to a lifetime of benefits.

I hope you see by now that the momentum of Cumulative Advantage can begin with the right opportunistic spark and the determination to act on an idea.

Here's the challenge for anybody in this time-starved, goal-oriented society: How do we take the time—even *schedule* the time—to explore things that are not directly related to our immediate goals?

Innovation can be a purposeful activity, but you need to take your eyes off the task at hand in order to connect with the new possibilities all around you. This is a challenge because most of us are wired to stay focused on the immediate needs of our jobs and families.

There's something satisfying about predictable, steady progress. But if you don't methodically act on your curiosity by connecting to new people, places, and experiences, you'll certainly miss the chance to uncover those random sparks that lead to success.

Being aware of the changes going on around you and connecting the dots can lead to big ideas. But is the timing of your idea right?

We can learn a lesson about that from the sport of American football.

# THE SEAM

*"Speed is the essence of war."*

—SUN TZU, *THE ART OF WAR*

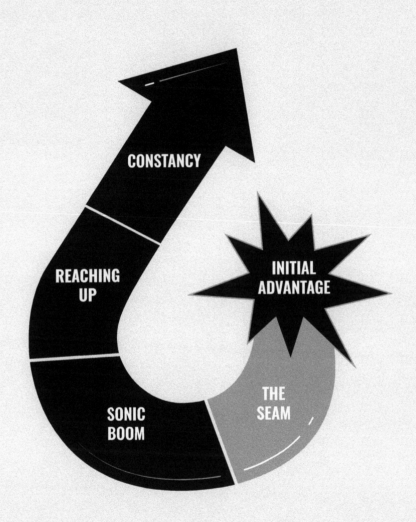

# CHAPTER 4

# THE SEAM

Harvard Professor Michael Porter is the author of 20 best-selling books including *Competitive Advantage*, one of the most important and revered business books of all time.

A six-time winner of the annual McKinsey Award for the best *Harvard Business Review* article, Professor Porter is the most cited author in the fields of business and economics.[1]

This man is a certified genius, and his path-finding books were the standard texts on business strategy for more than a decade.

In November 2012, Monitor Group, the consulting firm Porter co-founded, was unable to pay its bills and filed for bankruptcy. Ironically, Monitor's claim to fame was that it could help companies implement Porter's theory of "sustainable competitive advantage" and enjoy long-term profits.

This was Michael Porter, the sovereign of business strategy. How could it possibly go so wrong?

Hundreds of articles and several books have documented the shocking demise of this celebrated consultancy. The core problem was that Porter's classic idea of sustainable competitive advantage prescribes a *stationary* mindset.

According to this much-trusted model, once you've found a sustainable advantage, your job is done. Theoretically, you sit back and enjoy consistent profits because you've put the research and strategy into your Porter framework.

But business is *dynamic*, and the speed of change is accelerating. Forces of competition are constantly fluctuating. Competitors become more or less powerful, new entrants into the market change the rules, and technological shifts can alter the business landscape like a wild cyclone.

There's no such thing as a set-it-and-forget-it strategy anymore. Once you've established some small advantage, the momentum depends on what you do with it. You need to act before your relevance collapses.

## FINDING THE SEAM[2]

Today, businesses and entrepreneurs need an active framework for setting strategic direction more like American football. These teams fixate on exploiting any space on the field that is underdefended, even for an instant.

You don't have to be an American football fan to picture the strategy. Each team lines up against each other, face-to-face, strength against strength. To move the ball down the field, the team with control of the ball has to find some momentary opportunity ...

- Is there an imbalance between player defensive matchups to exploit?
- Is there a player on the other team who is inexperienced, slightly injured, or fatigued?
- Can our players find a weakness and pry open a space long enough to advance down the field?

In other words, the team tries to find an open seam, a vulnerability in the defense, that will work in that moment. Not tomorrow. Not next year. Right now.

Some coaches are watching the field from high above the game, urgently seeking a weakness, as are coaches on the field. Even players within the game gather in a huddle before every play to share information from the coaches and adjust their strategy.

In this analogy, success doesn't come from a 50-page document and a two-year plan. Strategy becomes any opportunity that exploits speed, time, and space. And once you break through, you build momentum that will take you as far as you can go, for as long as you can go!

A seam is an undefended—or underdefended—opportunity. It is a fracture in the status quo.

A common term for a new market or business opportunity is "finding a white space." A seam is a white space with urgency.

Like an elite athlete, once entrepreneurs find a seam, they need to accelerate to maximum speed and push that space forward for their benefit as long as possible. And then they need to look for the next seam.

Seams of opportunity exist everywhere in the business world, and the same football rules apply:

No seam, no gain.

Little seam, little gain.

Big seam, SCORE!

- Pinterest found an untapped market among women for sharing visual scrapbooks, scaled quickly, and became the third-biggest social network in just 18 months.

- Starbucks was a tiny company with no advantage in buying power or scale. They didn't invent coffee or the coffee shop, yet they found a seam—good-tasting coffee in a welcoming, conversational atmosphere—and burst through the opening with lightning speed.

- For nearly 30 years, Enterprise Rent-A-Car was the only company that picked up and dropped off local customers who needed a replacement vehicle. *Huge seam. Huge gain.*

If you dig deeply into the source of profitability for most companies today, you'll find that it's based on the fact that they've created a monopoly of time, space, or mindshare that is unassailable … at least for a period of time. A leader's role is to relentlessly search for the next undefended seam and help the organization burst through it with precise execution.

Fabio Tambosi, global head of brand communications for Adidas, told me that the most significant brand innovation today comes from leveraging "cultural creativity" with relevant micro consumer moments. "The most impactful marketing today is about finding the connective tissue between the intersection of brand values and what's happening in popular culture right now," he said. "Brands used to try to set 'bonfires'—multi-year campaigns. But today we're constantly looking for culturally relevant sparks. Great marketing is about leveraging the ripple effect of those continuous communication sparks."

In this new perspective, "brand-building" is a company's effort to extend a seam for as long as possible. By continuing to adjust a product's relevance and emotional connection to an audience, a marketing team can keep that seam open for decades and even widen that gap over time. In the case of iconic brands like Patagonia and Coca-Cola, they've dominated a seam and leveraged new ones for more than a century.

Brand expert Evelyn Starr commented: "At some point the brand can *become* the seam—it's an established position to be defended. There might be competitors, but the towering stance of a powerful brand makes it hard to replicate established, emotional relationships they have with their audiences. Those relationships can keep the seam open for decades."

In the first chapters of the book, I've used the sociological concept of Cumulative Advantage to describe how momentum works for new ideas and small businesses. McKinsey researchers showed how this works on a corporate level, too. Their study divided companies across 23 different industries into high-, medium-, and low-profit performers and then looked at their profitability over time.[3]

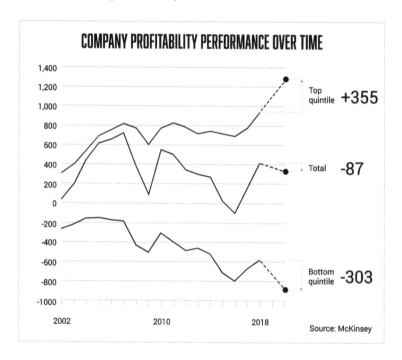

Over a period of 20 years, the companies in the top quintile of performers stayed at the top, the middle stayed more or less in the middle, and the bottom quintile took a slow road south through the years. Even through the rough recessionary years of 2009 and 2020, the rich got richer. The gap widened.

# FINDING YOUR SEAM

In Chapter 3, we discovered that randomness can be nurtured if we put ourselves in a place to find insight through a collision of people, places, and ideas.

Now we have to determine if that insight aligns with undefended opportunity. Can we pilot our idea through a seam?

A Bloomberg analysis found that of the 100 richest people in the world, eight had no college education or inherited family wealth—no obvious Cumulative Advantage. There was one common source of their unexpected success: Every one of them recognized an early trend and capitalized on the undefended opportunity by bursting through the seam.[4]

OK. I know you're dying to know who those eight billionaires are: Larry Ellison, Li Ka-shing, Leonardo Del Vecchio, John Fredericksen, Sheldon Adelson, Ingvar Kamprad, and Francois Pinault. No need to thank me.

New seams are opening always and endlessly. An undefended opportunity can come from changing customer needs, exploiting competitor laziness, specialized data analysis, or the application of a new technology. Seams emerge because of changes in buyer power, supplier power, availability of substitutes, or new rivalries. Seams open because of fluctuations in consumer tastes, culture, politics, fashion, and demographic trends.

For example, I used to be in the packaging business. Here's a fact everybody in the wine industry knows but will never admit: If you truly want to protect your product, the worst possible package is a transparent bottle with a cork closure.

For years I tried to convince winemakers of the benefits of packaging wine in aluminum cans. The industry collectively turned its nose up at the idea.

Guess what?

Wine in aluminum cans is now the fastest-growing product category in the industry, with a forecast that 10 percent of all wine sales will soon be in cans.[5]

Why? The can hasn't changed, but millennial consumers have different priorities. They're less interested in the emotion and tradition represented by a heavy bottle of wine and prefer the value of a small, light, quickly chilled package you can toss in a backpack. Such a simple and useful idea. An idea I had 20 years ago … but the seam had not opened yet. The idea had to be pulled through by a change in consumer tastes.

New opportunities are especially ripe in times of crisis, which are always a catalyst for underserved needs to materialize. In the 2020 pandemic, for example, there were astonishing new opportunities for food delivery, homeschooling help, and sanitizing supplies. Recessions hurt some businesses but build others. Some of the world's most successful companies, including Electronic Arts, IBM, and FedEx, were launched during economic downturns.

Is there a seam opening up right now for you and your ideas? To find out, there are three questions you need to answer:

1. Is the opportunity you've discovered undefended, or at least underdefended, in viable territory?

2. Is the opportunity a personal fit for you and your life?

3. Is the timing of the opportunity right?

Let's consider these one by one.

## 1. Have you found an undefended opportunity?

In 2011 when I was writing the *Return On Influence* book, I interviewed the venerable Harold Burson of Burson-Marsteller, a global PR firm he co-founded in 1953.

Mr. Burson is probably best known for helping companies manage through some of the worst PR nightmares in history, including an incident in 1982 when the Tylenol brand was nearly ruined by people tainting bottles with poison. A trusted brand had become a murder weapon ... and Harold helped the brand survive.

Mr. Burson died a few years ago, but when I met him, he was in his 80s and still energetically coming to work at 7 a.m. to write his memoir.[6] He told me his secret to a fulfilling life:

"During your life, many doors will open. The key to success is recognizing the right time to open those doors and the right time to close them."

Right on.

The trick is knowing which door to open, and that takes a little work. Somewhere between scribbling your idea on a cocktail napkin and launching your effort, you need to estimate your probability of success. It's easy to fall in love with an idea so thoroughly that you overlook the fact that perhaps nobody else cares about it! The number one reason for business failure is not enough demand for the new product or service.

In some cases, you may never know the true demand until you take the plunge. Or, maybe you'll get lucky and discover a use for your product or idea that you never knew existed. But if you're devoting a meaningful portion of your life to launching a new idea, why not give yourself the best chance to succeed and do some homework first?

That requires six considerations:

1. *Who are your potential customers?* Age, occupation, income, lifestyle, education, etc.

2. *What do they buy now?* Current buying habits relating to your product or service, including how much they buy, their favored suppliers, most popular features and the predominant price points.

3. *What will they buy in the future?* Ragy Thomas, founder of Sprinklr, told me: "Paint the picture of what the future can be, then work backwards. The best way to innovate is to think about the future backward, instead of the past forward. Startups often attempt to solve a problem that is occurring right now. Instead, entrepreneurs should build products and services around problems that will happen in the future and work backward to find solutions for those problems."

4. *Why do they buy?* This is a tricky but important question because ultimately your marketing depends on this answer. For example, you might be proud of the new functionality of your product, but people really buy it because it's a pretty color. Don't confuse what you sell with what people really buy.

5. *What will make them buy from you?* I encourage my clients to finish this sentence: "Only we …" Answering that is hard work, but if you align your meaningful points of differentiation with underserved customer needs, your probability of success skyrockets.

6. *Is our advantage defensible?* What competitors exist, and is our singular advantage significant enough to create a seam? Has there been a fracture in the status quo we can leverage?

We live in such an amazing information era, and perhaps 90 percent of the time you can do a suitable analysis on your own at little cost. The obvious first step is a thorough online search for data, but most cities also have small business development offices and entrepreneurial centers with abundant free or low-cost resources you can tap into.

But it's also important to just get out there and talk to potential customers. Important questions might include:

- What factors do you consider when purchasing this product or service?
- What do you like or dislike about current products or services currently on the market?

- What areas would you suggest for improvement?
- What is the appropriate price for this product or service?

Asking these questions on a regular basis can help you find a seam, and perhaps the next one, too! Some ideas are very low risk. Just go ahead and test the seam. But if building your dream involves a significant commitment of time and resources, don't take a shortcut on the research phase.

When I had the idea to write this book, I thought it was unique and could create an initial advantage that could build momentum for my business. In fact, a book always ignites a flurry of interest in my brand that leads to publicity, speaking engagements, workshops, and consulting jobs. But writing a book takes months of intense, dedicated effort. Publishing a book also represents significant risk to my reputation if I get it wrong! So I had to do some research on the seam:

- I searched Amazon for titles on this subject. There were no obvious competitors.
- I spent a few hours scanning published reports on the topic, and nearly all the work was academic. The idea of Cumulative Advantage had not crept into practical business applications. This was beginning to look like a legitimate seam for me.
- I started talking about the idea with trusted experts. They uniformly said the idea was "a big one" and a relevant topic for this time in history.

- With that encouragement, I took a deep plunge into the academic research to flesh out the original idea. (I was forming my initial advantage!)

- Over a period of months, I validated my ideas with friends and fans of my other books (potential customers) to refine my ideas.

- I wrote some blog posts articulating a few basic ideas and watched for feedback from people outside my circle of immediate friends.

Did I find an undefended opportunity? Time will tell, but I did the work.

## 2. Is the opportunity a personal fit for me and my life?

There are little ideas that improve a life and big ideas that change the world, but every idea requires some level of commitment. There has to be a *personal fit*.

"I've shelved so many ideas because my gut told me the product market fit wasn't right," said Mark Asquith, the co-founder of Rebel Base Media. "But it was the right idea and the right time—it was *me* that wasn't ready. There is a product fit but there also has to be a personal fit. I'd not walked the walk in the space I was entering enough to be able to know my potential customers. I had to become my customer for three years and then, after taking the ideas off the shelf, they flew!"

Another way to look at this idea of "personal fit" is through the lens of *ikigai*, an ancient Japanese ideology.

A combination of the Japanese words "iki," which means "life," and "gai," which is used to describe value or worth, ikigai is about finding meaning in life through purpose.

Your ikigai is what gets you up every morning and keeps your idea going.

The best way to illustrate the comprehensive nature of ikigai is by looking at a Venn diagram, which displays four overlapping qualities:

- What you're good at
- What the world needs
- What you can be paid for
- And of course, what you love

Boiling it down to its most basic theory, the central crossover of these points is where your ikigai—your purpose—resides.

Not only can ikigai provide some direction on the "fit" of your idea, but many sociologists believe this purposeful intersection can actually help you live longer.

A 2017 study of Kyotango, a small town in Kyoto with three times more residents over the age of 100 than normal, found that the elderly residents followed a daily routine supporting ikigai.[7]

Ani Alexander is a startup mentor and the London-based producer of my Marketing Companion podcast. She contends that this idea of "personal fit" is paramount for the timing of an idea: "If you move the idea aside and it keeps getting back to your head over and over again, if your idea keeps you awake at night, if you feel deep in your gut that if you don't do it you will always keep wondering what would have happened if you tried—then you better do it!"

In his landmark book *Innovation and Entrepreneurship*, Peter Drucker also discusses the need for "temperamental fit:"

> "Innovators need to be temperamentally attuned to the innovative opportunity. It must be important to them and make sense to them. Otherwise they will not be willing to put in the persistent, hard, frustrating work that successful innovation always requires."

Drucker says that this imperative applies on a corporate level. He points to an example where some pharmaceutical companies had been unsuccessful entering adjacent markets like skin care or cosmetics because they didn't fit the scientific temperament of the firm. In essence, a company has their ikigai, too.

When I was in graduate school, I learned an important lesson about the strategic fit of ideas from Hatim Tyabji, who was the CEO of Verifone at the time.

Verifone has long dominated the market for electronic point-of-sale transaction systems—those little boxes on sales counters used for authorizing credit card purchases. Since the late 1980s, Verifone has held more than 50 percent of the U.S. market for this product.

Hatim is among the most visionary and inspiring global leaders I've ever known, and he had some very strong ideas about the idea of "intra-preneurship."

"I do not believe there is any successful way to have a true entrepreneurial movement within a company," he told me. "If I would pit two competitors against each other—one working in the cozy confines of a company office and an independent person working out of their garage who will starve if they don't succeed—the garage person will always put in whatever work it takes to win.

"So my challenge was to reproduce that sort of momentum for a large company culture such as Verifone."

Hatim told me that he made an offer to anybody at Verifone who had a worthy entrepreneurial idea and a legitimate seam. He would provide initial financing and independent warehouse space for an office, but the innovator could no longer be a Verifone employee. No benefits, no salary, no safety net. They had to make the idea work like an independent entrepreneur.

The CEO named several success cases where Verifone bought key technologies developed by ex-employees, a win-win for both sides. The ex-employee became wealthy, and Verifone brought new ideas to market with cat-like entrepreneurial speed.

And speed is everything because timing is everything.

Once you've identified an initial advantage that solves a customer problem and aligns with "personal fit," how do you know if the timing of your idea is right?

That's a big question. And in the next chapter, I have a big answer.

# CHAPTER 5

# THE CERTAINTY OF UNCERTAINTY

In the mid-1980s, I worked on my first product launch ... and it was a big one! It was *literally* a launch, as in a NASA rocket rising into the sky.

My company at the time, Alcoa, had spent years researching a new market opportunity to manufacture small "dish" receivers that could attach to a home and pick up television broadcasts via space satellites.

The company had signed a partnership deal with one of the leading electronics companies in the world, NEC of Japan, who would provide the internal components for this groundbreaking product. NEC, a meticulous and thorough company like we were, had also spent millions of dollars on their own research confirming this market opportunity.

Between the two companies, we literally had truckloads of data proving that satellite dish TV would be a disruptive competitor to cable and a preferred technology in areas where cable was unavailable. The entry barriers were so high that this was an undefended opportunity! It was time to charge through the seam.

As a young marketing professional, I couldn't imagine anything more exciting! The combination of television and space satellites seemed as sexy as it was ever going to get for a guy working at a B2B metals company.

The data was unassailable. The projections showed endless rows of "hockey sticks," promising years of profits ahead for the partnership ... and I was in the middle of it.

But at 11:39 a.m. on January 28, 1986, America experienced one of the most gut-wrenching tragedies in its history. With millions of children watching the journey of Christa McAuliffe, the first schoolteacher to go to space, the Space Shuttle Challenger rose majestically into the cloudless Florida sky and broke apart into a firey ball just 73 seconds into its flight.

I'll never forget that moment and the tears that rolled down my face. The dramatic footage played over and over on the news. The image of that explosion is seared on my soul and the soul of our nation.

The Challenger was carrying our TV satellite in its payload.

The Space Shuttle program was put on hold for 32 months after this disaster. Alcoa projected that it could be 10 years before the satellite network could be launched again.

My company terminated the five-year development project and decoupled the partnership with NEC.

Eventually, "dish TV" became a reality. Alcoa didn't capture any of the business, but they had been right—it was a hit, with 34 million U.S. households owning the small receivers at the peak of the trend.

The point of the story is that despite years of planning and research and millions spent on development and partnerships, introducing any new idea carries massive uncertainty.

Alcoa's project fell victim to a heartbreaking accident. Ironically, another company I love owes its *success* to an accident.

## TWITTER QUAKE

Twitter was an internal side project of a startup called Odeo. Odeo was envisioned to be the ultimate homeroom for podcasts, but when Apple launched iTunes in 2005, the promising seam evaporated in a single day.

The founders of Odeo needed a new idea—fast!—and the leading candidate was a little texting service employee Jack Dorsey had been noodling over for the better part of a decade.[1]

Odeo launched Twitter in the spring of 2006, but despite heavy promotion and the strong backing of investors, the app attracted less than 500 users in its first year. Time was running out.

At 8:04 p.m. on October 30, 2007, the Alum Rock earthquake rattled Twitter's home base of San Francisco. The quake measured 5.6—the strongest earthquake to hit the Bay Area in nearly 20 years.

Luckily, the quake didn't cause extensive damage, but it was big enough to knock out power and many phone services. Suddenly the population of Northern California turned to Twitter for status updates on damage and aftershocks. Within two days, Twitter grew from a few hundred users to tens of thousands of users. The rest is history—the little blue bird eventually found its way into the hearts of millions of fans and a $5 billion valuation.

Side note: Did you know I wrote the best-selling book on Twitter?[2] It's rather unnerving to realize my career has been dramatically shaped by a spacecraft explosion and an earthquake.

## TIMING IS EVERYTHING

These stories demonstrate how predicting the ideal timing for an idea can be perilous! In the Alcoa example, a promising seam looked like it was 100 percent assured. With Twitter, a seam literally opened up with a crack in the earth.

There is *significant uncertainty* regarding any disruptive idea, and yet timing is undeniably important. When I talk about the right timing of an idea, it's not about launching in either this quarter or that quarter. It's about knowing when to charge through your seam when the conditions of an industry and a culture are right—something that usually can't be controlled or, in many ways, defined.

In a famous TED talk, entrepreneur Bill Gross provided an analysis of hundreds of startups and why they succeeded. The primary cause for an idea taking off as a successful business?[3] Timing: 42 percent of the successes were dependent on the right timing compared to 32 percent for execution and 28 percent for the uniqueness of the idea.

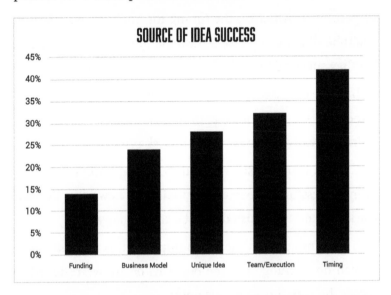

Bill pointed to unexpected successes like Airbnb and Uber (companies that were passed up by many smart investors). Both companies started during a recession when people needed to find sources of extra income—great timing.

"We started a company called Z.com—an online video entertainment company," he said. "We were so excited about it because we had raised enough money and we had a solid business model. We even signed great Hollywood talent to join the company.

"But broadband penetration was too low in 2000. And it was too hard to watch video content online because of the technical problems. The company went out of business in 2003.

"Just two years later, when the technical problem was solved by Adobe Flash and broadband penetration crossed 50 percent in America, the timing for YouTube was perfect. YouTube didn't even have a business model when it started, but they survived because the timing was so right."

If you're obsessed with an idea, it can be hard to accept that something so mysterious as timing can make or break you. Swing too early or too late and you risk missing the seam.

Clayton Christianson called this *The Innovator's Dilemma*. Even successful companies often fail with new ideas because markets that never existed can't be easily analyzed.[4]

If the timing of an idea is so important, is there *anything* we can do to nudge fortune our way, or are we resigned to accept the certainty of uncertainty?

## WORTHINESS

After reading dozens of case studies, books, and entrepreneurial epistles about the art and science of launching ideas, I've concluded that momentum begins when a worthy idea meets ideal timing. We may not be able to control timing, but we can certainly influence the "worthy" part. We can reduce uncertainty and tip the odds in our favor by focusing on "worthiness."

Now, "worthiness" is a gigantic, judgment-filled concept. But I think the deepest meaning of the word can either unlock a disruptive idea or heave it back on the shelf.

Is it the right time to launch? We can figure that out by answering these questions:

1. Is your idea worthy of a customer?
2. Is it worthy of a battle?
3. Is it worthy of the truth?

## 1. Is your idea worthy of a customer?

I love this quote from Tom Peters as he revealed the inspiration for his landmark book *In Search of Excellence*:

> "I didn't know what I was doing when I wrote Search. I wasn't trying to fire a shot to signal a revolution. But I did have an agenda. My agenda was this: I was genuinely, deeply, sincerely, and passionately pissed off! So what's the point? Just this: Nearly 100 percent of innovation—from business to politics—is inspired not by "market analysis" but by people who are supremely pissed off by the way things are.[5]"

Tom uses an important word here that is obviously missing from my list of "worthy" questions—passion.

I'm assuming that you wouldn't even think about launching an idea unless you're passionate about it. You're losing sleep over it. People claim you're obsessed over it. It won't ever leave your mind. You're drawing it. You're singing it.

My philosopher/mentor Robert Crosby once told me that there's no such thing as a weakness, just an overdone strength. There's a lot of wisdom in that notion.

Confidence is a strength, but overdone, it becomes arrogance.

Determination is a strength, but overdone, it turns into obsession.

And passion is a strength, too.

But too much passion can blind you to reality, and that's the primary problem I see among people with big ideas. Their idea becomes about *them and their ego* instead of the people the idea is supposed to serve.

I have a place on my website where anybody can sign up for an hour of my time. I've done hundreds of personal consulting sessions over the years, and a common issue I encounter is an entrepreneur pursuing an idea that solves no obvious problem. But they love the idea so much they can't see the plain truth. They don't even want to hear the truth. Any naysayer is simply an unwelcome "hater."

Blind belief in an idea can quickly destroy a project, according to Caroline McCullough, community manager for AquaLAB. "You know the time is right when you actually listen to what people say is important to them," she said. "Idea validation has an inherent problem in that it looks for agreement rather than opportunity. If you're listening for opportunity, it will be clear when the time is right because it will come from the very people you want to serve."

Mark Hood, managing director at Grow-Sure, said smart innovators have to fight past rose-colored glasses to see the truth in any idea. "Don't confuse 'would you' with 'will you,'" he said. "Would you buy this new sports car? Yes, I would. I would look great in that car! But *will* you buy it? No. It's too expensive and it can't tow my boat. Product timing is about doing your best to be relevant to the true needs of a market, not what you wish the market would be."

To achieve momentum, an idea must be simple and focused on one customer problem. It should do only one thing; otherwise it confuses people. The greatest feedback you could ever hear is: "This is so obvious. Why didn't I think of that?"

Bill Gross said, "Teams and execution definitely matter a lot, the idea matters a lot, but timing matters the most. And the best way to assess timing is to really look at whether consumers are ready for what you have to offer and be really honest about it. You can't be in denial simply because you have a product you love."[6]

Is your idea worthy of a customer and their true, current needs?

## 2. Is it worthy of a battle?

Launching an idea is sometimes like preparing for a long backyard brawl. No matter how sure you are about your seam, uncertainty is bound to catch up to you and throw a wrench in your momentum at the worst possible time.

Peter Drucker used to tell us in his class, "It's OK to fail, but never fail so hard that you're in a hole you can never get out of. Successful innovators are conservative. They're not risk-focused. They're opportunity-focused."

It's important to create a safety buffer around your idea so you don't fall too hard. Do you have the connections, resources, financing, and people to give yourself the best chance to succeed? Or, will you be so overextended that you're placing all future efforts at risk?

There has been a boatload of content created about this survival concept, most notably the idea of the minimum viable product, or MVP, led by Eric Ries,[7] so I have no need to expound on it here. The main concept is to have a practical battle plan so you can test the seam without sinking the lifeboat.

Eric contends that building momentum means that you don't just jump on an idea—you manage through it. Success requires starting small with as little investment and as few people as necessary. Otherwise, it's difficult to make the adjustments needed to make an idea soar.

"As you work through an idea you'll always face headwinds," said Christy Soukhamneut, chief of staff/director at Flagstar Bank. "As you adjust, enhance, and change, you'll notice that the headwinds get stronger or weaker. As the headwinds start to subside, you know the timing for the idea is spot on."

Alexandra Kunish, an instructor at Rutgers University and a former brand manager at Johnson & Johnson, added,

"Being second or third to a market is almost like borrowing experience from the pioneer. You can see the product, what works, what doesn't, consumer reaction, reviews, pricing and then improve upon it."

Ideal timing means you've prepared yourself for a sustained battle with uncertainty. Are you ready for the fight?

## 3. Is it worthy of the truth?

One of the biggest entrepreneurial failures of my life came because I ignored the truth.

For years I toyed with an idea of systematically amplifying the enormous amount of quality content created at company and association events. I sensed the seam for this was real because I was speaking at these conferences every week and observing that organizers didn't have the ability to staff an effective "newsroom" for real-time social media content.

But life got in the way. It was an idea in my notebook and nothing more. Coincidentally, years later I was approached by an entrepreneur who had the very same idea. He proposed an alliance.

The young man had some experience in the space and a tremendous amount of passion for the project. I fell in love with the notion of finally creating momentum around a beloved idea and a high-potential seam.

The problem was, I knew my new partner didn't have the resources lined up to pursue the fight. It would take two years to build this business. He had six months of funding available and his first baby on the way. Danger, Will Robinson!

Naturally, he burned through his cash and our startup crashed in six months.

Listen to both your heart and your head! Successful innovators use both the left and right sides of their brains. They pay attention to great people, but they also respect the analytics and the facts. In this case, I ignored both facts and my intuition.

Lindsay Tjepkema, CEO of Casted, notes the importance of intuition when your experience is close to a new idea. "Intuition is critical when it comes to timing," she said. "Not because of magic or stars aligning or crystals, but because my intuition is the supercomputer storing files and bits of data collected from all the years I've been on this planet. It's constantly retrieving information and honing my expertise and, most importantly, *it is unique to me.*

"The biggest challenge for an entrepreneur is knowing when to trust intuition. Why? Because others will question it and knock it down. But only I have the perfect information served up by my own experiences. When my intuition says the time is right, it's up to me to trust it and not let fear get in the way of opportunity."

In today's world, it's often more important to be fast than right, especially if the risk and entry barriers are low. Don't overthink things and let a seam close up on you. Intuition is valuable.

# THE MIGHTY ITERATION

Just because a market seems crowded or mature, that doesn't mean it's not ripe for disruption. The most promising seams can occur when competitors are unaware or lazy.

Most successful innovations come from followers who create iterations of existing ideas. The iPod transformed the delivery of music to consumers, but it wasn't the first MP3 player. It wasn't even the second or third. But because it was an iteration that placed a music ecosystem in your pocket, the timing was perfect.

"As soon as we have a great idea, we google it," said April Sciacchitano, co-founder of Mix+Shine Marketing and PR. "And usually, we find a competitor. Our immediate reaction is to think our timing is too late. It's already been done. But actually what we've found is an emerging or proven market. Being second or third? That might be incredible timing for an idea."

Timing is essential. Timing is elusive. But if you focus on the concepts in these last two chapters and build momentum for ideas that are:

1.  Focused on customer needs

2.  Aligned with personal and professional "fit"

3.  Consistent with data and market truth

… you'll be in the best position to take advantage of a seam at the right time.

So far, we have our worthy idea, we've hit our seam, and we're ready to roll ahead. But before we head down the next step of our journey toward Cumulative Advantage, let's consider how timing impacted the momentum paths of Ferriss and Schaefer.

# I SWERVE OFF COURSE

Tim has often said that the timing of his book "was perfect" for a generation burned out and worried about the impact of a world financial crisis.

Here was his seam: Tim's generation didn't have a guru.

In an article in *The New Yorker*, Rebecca Mead writes that every generation gets the self-help guru it deserves.[8]

In 1937, at the height of the Depression, Napoleon Hill wrote *Think and Grow Rich*, which claimed to distill the principles that had made Andrew Carnegie so wealthy, despite the fact that Hill never actually met Carnegie. A frightened and desperate country was willing to overlook the fact that the man was a complete fraud and elevate him as perhaps the first self-help authority.[9]

*The Power of Positive Thinking*, published by Norman Vincent Peale in 1952, advised readers that techniques such as "a mind-emptying at least twice a day" would lead to success.

By the 1970s, Werner Erhard and his mysterious "est" process promised material wealth through spiritual enlightenment.

The '80s and '90s saw management-consultancy maxims married with New Age thinking in books such as Stephen R. Covey's *The 7 Habits of Highly Effective People.*

In the past decade, there has been a rise in books such as *Who Moved My Cheese?* by Spencer Johnson, which promises to help readers maximize their professional potential in an era of unpredictable workplaces.

Ferriss' books appeal to those for whom cheese, per se, has ceased to have any allure.

"This book is not about finding your dream job," Ferriss writes. "I will take it as a given that, for most people, somewhere between six and seven billion of them, the perfect job is the one that takes the least amount of time."

But Ferriss doesn't recommend idleness. Rather, he prescribes a kind of hyperkinetic optimization of the body and soul, with every person serving as their own life coach, angel investor, web master, personal trainer, and pharmaceutical test subject. His books seem to have resonated with a particular *Wired*-reading, Clif Bar-eating man who finds in Ferriss the promise of heightened braininess complemented by an enviable degree of brawniness.

Tim accelerated through his bro seam with a blinding burst of speed and just kept running. The perfect idea at the perfect time. Big seam. Undefended opportunity. Touchdown!

What about Team Schaefer?

My key insight—generated from randomness, of course— was that the business world was changing rapidly, and power was shifting from media giants to digital natives publishing their views on anything and everything. We were on the verge of an influencer marketing revolution and almost nobody realized it.

To show you that the world was still asleep on this idea, here's a Google Trends chart showing the relative search volume for the term "influencer marketing" since 2012:

The obvious trend popping out here is that interest in influencer marketing is stretching toward the sky like July sunflowers on the Nebraska prairie. In my book, I predicted that within two years, this idea would take off and become a mainstream marketing staple … and I was right.

In fact, not to brag or anything, but I was *exactly* right … to my detriment. My seam for influencer marketing was two years away from the publication of my book. Yes, there was an undefended opportunity, and I burst through with full force. But, bad news—nobody was on the other side to greet me!

The mass market for my idea was still years away. It's amazing that the book sold as well as it did (we'll cover the reason for that in the next chapter).

For the first time, we see how my path began to swerve away from Oprah. Tim's timing was exactly right, but mine was years too early for mass-market acceptance.

This is a key lesson about timing. Your innovation has to address a clear and present problem.

It took 25 years for the computer to find a mass market, but the earliest developments of the technology still had immediate applications for accounting, scientific calculations, and simulations.

A little-known fact is that development of the light bulb began 10 years before Thomas Edison assembled his first team for the project. He waited until the timing was right and enough research, knowledge, and market pull was available to create a product that could be practical in the present, not the far-off future. When the timing was right, he poured everything he had into it.

I don't have any regrets about my timing. In fact, the timing was spot-on for me because *that's when I had the book deal.* I wasn't exactly going to say to McGraw-Hill, "No, let's wait because I have a hunch about this." And who could have known for sure that the influencer market momentum was still two years away?

**Timing is EVERYTHING.**

Tim had it. I didn't.

But I did have a sonic boom …

# THE SONIC BOOM

*"There is only one thing worse than being talked about, and that is not being talked about."*

—OSCAR WILDE

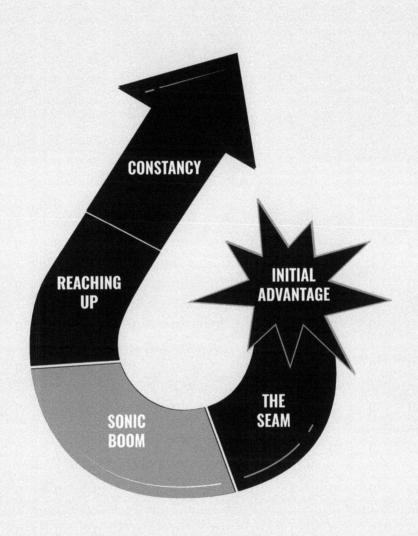

CONSTANCY

REACHING
UP

INITIAL
ADVANTAGE

SONIC
BOOM

THE
SEAM

## CHAPTER 6

# THE SONIC BOOM

During the 2020 pandemic lockdown, Serlina Boyd was looking for anything to keep her bored children occupied in her London flat. The usual games and videos were getting stale, so she ventured out to a newsstand to buy children's magazines for her 6-year-old daughter Faith.

When they started reading through the magazines together, Serlina realized that none of the children in the periodicals looked like Faith or her friends. There was a massive lack of diversity and representation in this mainstream media.

This became the initial spark for an improbable idea: launching two new print magazines in the middle of an economic crisis: *Cocoa Girl* and *Cocoa Boy* for Black kids aged 7-14.

Serlina had a small amount of experience with a previous magazine launch. She was on the team that helped design *Vera*, the inflight magazine for Virgin Airlines, and she's a talented graphic artist. But even with this background, *Cocoa Girl* seemed like a risky venture.

Due to the pandemic and her limited funds, any kind of true market research was out of the question. Friends and mentors were mixed about the notion of launching a new print magazine in an era where print is dying. One of her mentors flatly urged against it, telling her nobody would care about it.

The seam wasn't obvious, but the risk was low, so Serlina charged ahead anyway. Her plans to open a new childcare center had been jeopardized by the global health crisis, so her obsession and purpose, her ikigai, turned to bringing *Cocoa Girl* to life.

With the lockdown restrictions, Serlina was unable to recruit outside help for the magazine's launch, so she roped in her photographer husband and used her daughter as the face of the first *Cocoa Girl*. She convinced editor friends to help guide her through the first edition … all through remote collaboration.

The first edition was beautiful and inspiring, featuring sections on learning, fashion, crafts, gardening, and Black history. She was confident about finding an audience. "I don't think print is dead … it's the content being put out there that's dead," she said.

Serlina had already penciled in an official launch date for the magazine, but civil unrest in the United States catapulted race issues into the media spotlight around the world. She realized that her publications could be more relevant than ever. Perhaps the timing was perfect.

In anticipation of the official launch, Serlina put the covers of *Cocoa Girl* and *Cocoa Boy* on her Facebook page with a link in hopes of generating her first orders.

And then ... the media discovered her. Here's what happened after her first Facebook post:

## Week One

- A small notice of the magazine launch appeared in the Fashion + Beauty Monitor.
- An article in London's *Mirror* newspaper (circulation 500,000) received more than 20,000 social shares.

## Week Two

- The magazine launch was covered by ITV London News.
- The BBC did a special primetime segment on the innovative magazine launch.

## Weeks Three and Four

- A video report was created by Yahoo! News, providing global coverage for a magazine that had just launched its first edition out of a London apartment.
- *Access Hollywood* profiled Serlina and her new magazine.

… and so on.

Serlina couldn't control most aspects of timing that contributed to her success. However, her idea passed the "worthiness test" from Chapter 5:

1. Focused on customer needs
2. Aligned with personal and professional "fit"
3. Consistent with data and market truth

… so she was prepared to ride the crest of the wave. The media attention made her little magazine—with just one issue under her belt—nearly ubiquitous.

Within three weeks, Serlina Boyd had a blockbuster business on her hands. "My phone didn't stop going off with all the sales," she said. "I was selling a magazine a minute."

She sold 20,000 subscriptions in the first few weeks and was awarded in-store sales contracts at retailers like Waitrose and WHSmith within six months. The momentum is carrying her and her family into a new level of financial success.

## THE CUMULATIVE ADVANTAGE BOOST

Let's go back to the original concept of Cumulative Advantage. Those with some kind of head start—education, wealth, resources, or connections—will keep widening their advantage unless you get a boost through *countervailing processes*.

Serlina had no obvious claim to Cumulative Advantage with her magazine project. In fact, the odds seemed stacked against her success:

- Print magazines were dying.
- She had almost no firsthand experience in marketing or publishing a magazine.
- Her professional connections were against the idea.
- She had to bootstrap every aspect of production from her apartment.
- The economy was in an unprecedented freefall during a pandemic.

So, she needed a boost, and she received it from a windfall of media coverage.

If Serlina continues to execute well, there's no reason to believe her success won't continue to compound and eventually extend into international markets. She has achieved the early momentum of Cumulative Advantage!

I'm not saying everybody needs a massive media boost like this to have a successful business or product launch. Almost nobody has luck like that! But to achieve unstoppable momentum, you need to create awareness for your idea.

Specifically, you need a sonic boom.

## BUSINESS IS BOOMING

For many years, one of my favorite marketing thought leaders has been Steve Rayson. Steve founded a number of successful companies, sold them, became wealthy, and went on to pursue an academic career in political science. But during his tenure leading a company called BuzzSumo, he had an esteemed track record of publishing remarkable and useful research.

A core competency of the BuzzSumo technology is finding patterns among the millions of pieces of content published on the web every day.

In one of my favorite articles, Steve explained how "going viral" isn't exactly what everybody thinks it is.

You might imagine that an idea spreads through a network that looks like a spiderweb—one person shares it, then a friend shares it, then somebody from that new network shares it, and on and on.

But that's not what Steve discovered at all. Through complex statistical analysis, he could show that an idea catches on when a number of powerful social media accounts all post about it at the same time. This creates what I've called a "sonic boom" in my marketing workshops and lectures, and this is a primary strategy to achieve launch velocity for an idea.

Steve explained that when *more than one* powerful and trusted "influencer" shares content, the number of resulting social media shares goes up. A validation effect of some kind occurs. If one influential person or company posts about your idea, OK … but if people are seeing it everywhere, then it MUST be something important. The trust in the content is secured, and the idea is shared.

As more influential people share an idea, the number of social shares and reposts grows exponentially, like a drop of oil spreading over a puddle.

- Posts that were shared by two influencers had 30 percent more shares than a post shared by a single influencer.

- Posts that were shared by three powerful people received more than 100 percent more shares.

- Posts that were shared by five people received nearly *300 percent* more shares.

Five seemed to be the magic number for critical mass. If you can get as few as five relevant and influential accounts spreading one idea, you're on your way towards creating a sonic boom. Here's a graph from the BuzzSumo research:

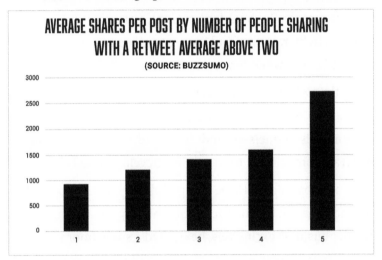

Steve told me that this research became the foundation of his company's content marketing strategy: Find a way to get at least five relevant influencers to share every research report they published.

Now, there is always considerable work required when choosing exactly the *right* influencers who are established and relevant, but certainly this is a powerful and effective strategy, and it's worked for me and many others I've counseled over the years.

It even helped launch my favorite bike helmet.

# TOUR DE FORCE

For many years I was an enthusiastic mountain biker until ... well, let's say my "center of gravity" shifted! But I still love to get out on my bike, and my helmet of choice for many years has been Giro.

Before I found Giro, the helmets I had were boxy and uncomfortable. But founder Jim Gentes came up with a design that was lighter, stylish, and more aerodynamic. It was the first helmet I ever owned that came close to being "cool."

In the early days of his business, Jim crafted these pioneering helmets by hand in his garage. By attending bike events and showing his helmets around, he found enough early fans to generate some orders to sustain his developmental efforts.[1]

Jim probably could have bumped along with this "boutique" business model, but in order to quit his day job and pursue his helmet business exclusively, he needed a sonic boom.

He studied how Nike commonly used influential athletes to create viral content about new product ideas. He thought that if he could get Tour de France competitors to wear his teardrop-shaped Aerohead helmet, both pros and serious amateur cyclists would want to wear his helmet too, starting a cascade of influence.

Jim bet the meager resources of his company on this one idea, sponsoring several professional cyclists, including American Greg LeMond. In the dramatic finale of the 1989

Tour de France, LeMond overcame a 50-second deficit at the start of the time trial to win the entire 23-day, 2,000-mile race by 8 seconds.

Wearing a Giro.

Suddenly, it became *very cool* for serious riders (and even me) to wear the aerodynamic Giro helmet!

Today, Giro is a multi-million-dollar company with product extensions into every aspect of cycling gear and high-performance downhill skiing accessories, all launched with their own athlete-oriented sonic booms.

## HELLO, MS. KING!

Let's return to our Ferriss-Schaefer case study and see how sonic booms affected our relative momentum.

When we last left our race toward Oprah Town, both contestants had even prospects, a good idea that represented an initial advantage, and a book deal.

Tim was probably pulling ahead of me when it came to timing. As I explain in Chapter 5, my idea about influence marketing was ahead of its time, so Tim had found a bigger audience ready for his idea.

Both of us had publishing deals, but here's where I pull ahead again.

Remember, Tim had been rejected 26 times. He was finally picked up by Harmony Publishing, a small subsidiary of Crown/Penguin Publishing dedicated to wellness books.

I was courted by several publishers who were in a bidding war for my book. I chose McGraw-Hill, one of the world's most respected publishers with a gleaming New York City office tower near Rockefeller Center. McGraw-Hill had been publishing books since 1888. They knew what they were doing.

Both Tim and I were relative unknowns at that time. We both really needed a sonic boom.

McGraw-Hill got to work and soon had me lined up for interviews up and down the spine of Manhattan: Bloomberg News. *The Wall Street Journal. The New York Times.*

And then I got the big call.

It was a glorious spring day in New York City, and I decided to walk back to my hotel after a strenuous day of promotional interviews. I was rambling down a shady, tree-lined street in Chelsea when my editor called and told me that a limousine would pick me up at 6 a.m. the next morning for a live appearance on the CBS Morning News in front of an estimated four million viewers.

I was terrified.

Literally.

Terrified.

After a sleepless and queasy night, I arrived at the studio with one mission: Do not embarrass my wife, who had told all her friends I would be on the national news that morning.

After a little makeup treatment, I was escorted to the Green Room where I sat next to Eric McCormack, the excellent actor of Will and Grace fame. Obviously, we became BFFs.

And then Gayle King, one of the morning news hosts, came into the room to greet me and help me relax before my segment.[2]

"Mr. Schaefer!" she exclaimed brightly. "I LOVED your book! Every week they give us these business books to read for the show and I am always so bored with them, but I couldn't put your book down."

As proof, she showed me her copy of *Return On Influence,* which had been filled with sticky notes and yellow marker highlights. She really had read the whole book!

Now let's rewind for a moment because I forgot to fill you in on a crucial detail. *Gayle King is Oprah's best friend!*

In your face, Tim Ferriss.

I was that close. One degree of separation. I was very nearly in Oprah Orbit.

The interview went extremely well, I did not embarrass my wife, and I can say with certainty that Gayle King and the tsunami of press coverage I received that week created a sonic boom that propelled my book to the number one spot on the Amazon business book lists for six weeks.

Remember, I was a nobody. This was my first book. My momentum came from the boom and only the boom.

What about Tim?

He didn't have the backing of a McGraw-Hill ... he was lucky to have a book deal at all. So he had to start a sonic boom himself.

In a *New Yorker* profile, M.J. Kim, a New York publicist, fondly described Ferriss as "the smartest self-promoter I know."

M.J. recalled that shortly after they met, Ferriss asked her if he could piggyback the launch of The 4-Hour Workweek onto a birthday party she was throwing for herself. "It was ridiculous," she said. "While everyone was having cocktails and singing 'Happy Birthday,' he was handing out copies of his book. It was a case of 'Who is that guy?'"[3]

Pundits have compared Tim to P. T. Barnum, and he certainly has a skill for self-salesmanship. Tim not only worked the parties, but he also worked an emerging network of power bloggers.

Remember the timeframe: Tim's first book came out in 2009. Blogging was just gathering steam. There was no such thing as a social media "influencer" back then. Bloggers were the very first web content creators, and getting a book or a phone call from a *real author* was a big deal. A blogger trying to break through would do everything in their power to help that person ... and they did.

"Most publishers at the time were focusing on television interviews," Tim said. "But that content expires as soon as it comes out. One day ... and it's gone. There's no lasting benefit to that media exposure. Conversely, evergreen online content can appreciate over time."[4]

"My goal in the beginning was to find 20,000 'early-vangelists' (a term coined by Eric Ries). This is a very large and specific number," he said. "My thinking was that if you have 10,000 sales in a week you have a very good chance to hit a national best-seller list like *The Wall Street Journal* or *The New York Times*.

"You can't reach the whole world all at once. It's too expensive. So my target audience was 20-to-35-year-old tech-savvy male bloggers, and there were five or ten of them that I ended up targeting."

To enact his strategy, Tim attended the first-ever bloggers "Tweet Up" at the 2009 Consumer Electronics Show in Las Vegas and started passing out cards. "He had done his homework," one blogger remembered. "It was obvious that he had studied us. Read our blogs and tweets—he could start a conversation right away. We didn't know what he was doing there, but he was cool and smart and he ingratiated himself to us. A month later he sent all of us his book and asked for help, so of course we wanted to promote it. He understood the media of the day."

Tim said: "I wanted to create a surround sound effect … meaning that a typical book launch from a publisher focuses on four to eight weeks, and I wanted all my promotion to happen in one week. Through those bloggers, I wanted to be unavoidable to those 20,000 early adopters who I thought would like my book."

Sounds a lot like a sonic boom, doesn't it? Tim was able to produce enough momentum that he hit his 10,000-book goal. That convinced the publisher to invest in the book, propping it up on *The New York Times* best-seller list for four years.

My own business book was a hit, but it was nothing compared to Tim's (we covered the timing impact in Chapter 5). Neither one of us would have beat the odds on our first book without a sonic boom.

## SOCIAL PROOF, SONIC BOOM

The psychology behind the sonic boom is based on a very important marketing idea called *social proof*. This is a useful psychological process that you probably use every day. In the absence of facts, a person scans their environment for clues to help them make their best decision.

Let's say you and a friend want to find a new place for dinner. You walk into a restaurant and it's empty at 7 p.m. You get an uncomfortable feeling that maybe it's not the best choice. So, you walk across the street to your second option. The place is packed, and people are laughing and talking. You happily put your name on the list and wait 15 minutes for a table.

In this scenario, you don't have any facts about the quality of the food or service. You're making a decision entirely on an environmental clue—filled tables. That's social proof.

This invisible influence is always at work behind the scenes, silently pushing and pulling momentum in powerful directions.

For example, one of the persistent mysteries in the entertainment industry is how awful experienced industry executives are at picking hits. The top names in the business rejected and even disparaged smash hits like *Star Wars*, *Harry Potter*, and the Beatles, while many of their confident bets turned out to be duds.

How could the smartest and most experienced people in Hollywood be so dead wrong in their predictions?

Entertainment companies spend so much money on market research and creative development that it seems like they could figure out what it is about Taylor Swift that appeals to so many fans … and then replicate it. And indeed, that's pretty much what they try to do.

The problem is, most market research makes a huge assumption: When people make decisions about what they like, they do it independently of one another. But people almost never make decisions independently. The world abounds with so many choices that we have little hope of ever finding what we want on our own. So we rely on social proof.

## SOCIAL PROOF BEATS QUALITY EVERY TIME

Columbia University researchers showed that differences in popularity are incredibly sensitive to the Matthew Effect. The rich get richer, or in this case, the popular get *more* popular. They found that when content like a song, book, or movie is perceived to be even slightly more popular than another, it will build momentum and rise above the competition. Once again, advantage leads to advantage.

Even tiny, random fluctuations in early signs of popularity can blow up and go viral, generating potentially enormous long-run differences—even when the competitors might have more advantages than you!

To prove this, the researchers created an artificial web-based music market called Music Lab.[5] The site offered people an opportunity to hear 48 unknown songs by unknown bands.

Half of the 14,000 site visitors were invited to download their favorite songs, and it became obvious which of the 48 tunes were the "best."

The other 7,000 visitors were sorted into "social influence" groups, which were exactly the same with one difference: The groups rated songs after they observed how many times each song had been downloaded by other participants. In essence, social proof helped them decide their favorite songs.[6]

You might expect that quality would prevail—the very best songs would always rise to the top. But that isn't what happened. In short, everything hinged on initial popularity. Almost any song could do really well or really poorly *depending on what the social proof from others indicated.*

By exposing people to different sets of feedback, the researchers could manipulate which songs became popular regardless of quality, just as Cumulative Advantage theory would predict.

Overall, a song in the Top 5 in terms of quality (as determined by the independent group) had only a 50 percent chance of finishing in the Top 5 of success when social proof was added. Social proof played a larger a role than quality in determining the market share of successful songs.

The long-run success of a song depended heavily on the decisions of a few random, early-arriving voters.

But what if it wasn't random?

Think about the implications of this for your own ideas. What if you hand-select the early reviewers and they're people who love you and your work? We begin to see the psychological underpinnings of the sonic boom. If the earliest feedback on your idea is positive and shared widely, it's much more likely to create the momentum needed to take you to the top and keep you there.

This lesson is not limited to cultural products like songs and movies. Economists have shown that similar mechanisms affect the competition between technologies (like operating systems or social media sites) that display what are called "network effects"—the popularity of a product or idea increases with the number of people using it.

This is an important reality I explore in-depth in my book *Marketing Rebellion*. Today, the customer is the marketer. Company promotions and ads are becoming irrelevant because we avoid them and don't believe them anyway. People believe each other. Their friends. Neighbors. Technical experts. Business leaders. Influencers. The "early votes" of these people through reviews, testimonies, social media posts, and word of mouth have a disproportionate impact on momentum that leads to Cumulative Advantage.

Now, for the record, I do believe that quality matters. Mozart, Monet, Maya Angelou, and my beloved Bruce Springsteen were destined for success. If content is truly horrible, it's going to flop. But within a wide range of quality, a product or an idea can do very well or very poorly depending on the social proof that surrounds it.

Creating awareness for your ideas is important, but what we've covered here is just the tip of the iceberg. To earn your sonic boom, you probably need to pay your dues first. Next, I'll tell you why.

# CHAPTER 7

# PERSONAL VELOCITY

This book is meant to help you overcome some of the ways the world is stacked against you and create momentum for whatever you're passionate about, no matter who you are or where you come from.

In Chapter 6 I describe one proven technique—creating a sonic boom—that helps overcome disadvantage and creates awareness for a worthy idea or product.

But it occurred to me that even that concept assumes some pre-existing status. Tim Ferriss had built relationships with powerful bloggers who helped him boost his book. My book hype depended on connections from my experienced PR support team at McGraw-Hill. I benefited from having a book contract—and very few people would ever have that advantage.

Tim and I possessed inherent advantage in our own right.

But we're here to fight for the everyman and everywoman. How do you build Cumulative Advantage and earn a sonic boom from a standing start—with no inherent advantages?

To provide some guidance on that, I'll tell two short stories that will magically come together into one essential lesson. Here we go.

## STORY #1: THE MATTHEW EFFECT ON THE WEB

In 2014, I wrote the most impactful blog post of my career. It was called "Content Shock: Why Content Marketing is not a Sustainable Strategy," and it went nuts. I had thousands of social shares and comments. It was the very definition of viral! "Content Shock" eventually became a standard industry term that is commonly used in articles, conference presentations, and books.

In the article, I rationally pointed out that when we reach a point where there is too much competition in an industry niche, it's harder to stand out. Content marketing becomes more expensive and less effective. To me, this was common sense. But some people considered this a bombastic post. For the people who sell content marketing for a living, it was heresy.

Nevertheless, this is the type of viral exposure every business dreams about.

About three weeks after I wrote this post, I googled the term "Content Shock" to discover other commentary about my post. To my astonishment, my blog post came up *third* in the search results.

Wait … what?

There was no pre-existing SEO for "Content Shock." It was a term I just made up. How in the world could other articles already beat me in the search results?

It turns out the Matthew Effect is alive and well and living on the world wide web!

The most powerful content doesn't win on the web—the most powerful websites do. And that's what happened here. Websites that had been around far longer than mine with more prestige in the eyes of Google charged up the charts ahead of me, even though I had done all the work! Robert Merton is smiling down on us somewhere.

Organically winning the top search result slots is nearly impossible, especially if you're young, new, or inexperienced. In most categories, SEO is a battle between the two biggest, meanest junkyard dogs in your industry, constantly duking it out for the top search listings. Unless you're one of those dogs, your search future probably isn't bright.

The SEO people probably don't want you to hear this because they need you to buy their SEO services. But the fact is, the people who have already won a niche with their content are probably going to stay there for a long time, no matter how hard you work to unseat them. This is rarely an undefended opportunity.

The rich get richer.

And it gets worse.

Today, more than 50 percent of all search on the web stays with Google. It's not available to you and your company at all. Google sends the search traffic to one of its own properties or one of its paying customers. So even if you have a chance to win at SEO, the available inquiries on a topic are shrinking compared to even just a few years ago. And of course, those spots are dominated by the junkyard dogs anyway.

SEO is an important and evolving topic—far beyond the scope of this book—but I wanted to make the point that most of the time, even the internet is stacked against us.

To be clear, certainly there is a place for SEO in the world, and it's absolutely critical for some businesses. But for most of us, overcoming the inherent unfairness on the web requires another answer.

## STORY #2: THE OLD MAN AND THE BLOG

Over more than a decade, I've successfully built a personal brand—first through my blog, then through the Marketing Companion podcast, my books, and speeches I've given around the world. Through the popularity of my content, I haven't depended on the search engines to deliver customers and relevant new business connections. I've never even taken out an ad to promote my business.

But in this journey, I started at zero. Maybe less than zero.

My friend Mitch Joel, a Montreal-based entrepreneur, once told me, "When you started out, I predicted you would never make it. You were too old and too late. There were too many marketing bloggers already."

But I did indeed make it because it didn't matter that I was old or late. I just needed to be as consistent as The Black Keys.

The Black Keys are a super-charged, lo-fi, blues-infused, stomp machine of a band. When I first met founding members Patrick Carney and Dan Auerbach, they weren't playing stadiums and arenas like they are now. They were playing clubs that held less than 1,000 people. But they definitely had momentum.

I asked Patrick, the drummer for the group, what the ignition point had been. What was the one event or moment that seemed to boost their trajectory to the big time? This was a vital question for me as I was in the process of building my own digital marketing business.

His answer surprised me.

"There was no singular event," he said. "We just keep making steady progress. Each album does a little better than the last one. You just keep moving forward, building your audience one show at a time, week by week, and month by month."

If you study the band's career, this now seems obvious. It took seven albums and a decade of hard touring for the band to complete an improbable journey from basement recording project to arena-rock stardom. Three years after I met them in the back of an Asheville, NC, club that didn't even have any seats, The Black Keys sold out New York City's Madison Square Garden in less than 15 minutes.

Multi-platinum artist Kristian Bush, a founding member of the band Sugarland, told me a similar story:

"Everyone thinks our momentum started with a big hit, but it wasn't that way at all. Music business success comes from cumulative progress. There are two kinds of bands. One kind is the one-hit wonder. You don't want that. If that happens, you realize it would have been far more profitable to be an accountant instead. What I realized—especially in the country music industry—building momentum is progressive.

"The momentum really starts with the first song on the radio. It takes a lot of work to get there, but it opened every door. A second hit song proves that the first song wasn't a fluke. But at that point, people still love the song ... not you. They're not attached to you because they don't know who you are yet.

"As the momentum builds you become associated with a song and a sound and a story. Sugarland songs have a certain emotional temperature, a moral center, a compass, and of course the pleasure of hearing Jennifer Nettles as a singer. Momentum builds from just being consistent and focused. Familiarity breeds familiarity."

So what does this mean to you and me?

As I consider the people who are making a name for themselves in the world today, there is not one person who was "an overnight success." Social media pioneer Chris Brogan once famously said that it took him three years to get his first 100 blog readers. But a few years later, he was the leading speaker in the business.

Here is a chart depicting the number of subscribers to my blog since 2013 (I actually began blogging in 2009 but no longer have the data):

**BLOG SUBSCRIBERS**

Slow and steady. Each year is a little better than the last. Just like The Black Keys and Sugarland and Chris Brogan.

The trendline for my podcast downloads and book sales looks the same way.

Whether you're a band or a blogger, it's unlikely that you'll experience a "viral event" that puts you on a path of fame and fortune. You establish your voice, create content, and keep grinding it out until you become "a song and a sound and a story."

"Consistent effort is everything," said Maria A. Rodriguez, a marketing director and content marketing strategist. "I fell in love with social media and influencer marketing because it provides an opportunity for everybody.

"I grew up in Colombia, a country where job opportunities are scarce. My parents didn't have the connections or network that can help you when you are trying to break into a specific industry. I was young and didn't have any experience … didn't have much of anything. But I saw my opportunity in content creation.

"I used my journalism degree to learn how to tell stories on my own using digital technologies. I started interviewing people and sharing that content online. I thought this was a way to show people what I could do. A producer eventually found my content, liked what I was doing, and hired me to work in broadcast television. That led to additional exposure, a scholarship at an American university, and new job opportunities. It's how I earned the job I have now.

"My career momentum came from using the free internet tools available to me and never giving up. You can't expect things to just come to you. You're not going to be an overnight sensation. Keep working and the doors start to open for you."

The closest I ever came to being an overnight sensation was the Content Shock article I mentioned. It was published in early 2014 and if you look at the early part of the graph you can see the impact it had on my subscribers—none! There's *no substitute for consistent, steady progress.*

I didn't have a paying sponsor for my Marketing Companion podcast until year three. I didn't make noticeable money on my books until my fifth publication, The Content Code, in year six of my "second career." I struggled for three or four years before booking speaking gigs that paid meaningful money.

Consistency is more important than genius.

# BRINGING THE STORIES TOGETHER

The point of Story #1 is that it's dreadfully difficult to stand out on the web and build momentum if you depend on Google, Facebook, or any other tech company to pull you along.

The implication of Story #2 is that you don't necessarily need Google anyway. You can rely on yourself by generating an initial advantage through your own creativity and resilience. I generated my own momentum because I was driven to do so, and I didn't give up.

Now let's connect the meaning of these stories to the sonic boom in Chapter 6.

When I was starting out, my audience was small, my influence puny, and my ability to call in favors from powerful influencers nonexistent.

But as the number of subscribers slowly rose upward, my ability to influence larger crowds of more important people rose, too. The number of subscribers I attracted is a good proxy for my influence.

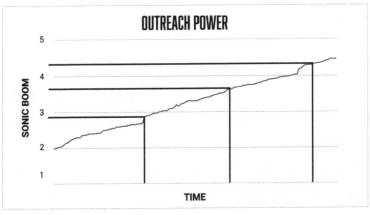

This illustration is an imaginary "power grid" superimposed on the first chart of my subscriber growth. The grid is theoretical, but the reality is true. The more momentum I had, the more power I had to ask for favors. When I started from scratch I had absolutely no ability to create even a sonic whimper. After a few years, maybe I could make a sonic murmur. But my promotion potential grew as long as I kept plugging away.

I'm still not where I want to be. I wrote my hero, the wonderful writer-philosopher Brené Brown, and asked if I could interview her for this book. Her assistant got back to me after a few weeks and politely declined. By the way, Brené was recently a guest on the Tim Ferriss podcast. Naturally.

Advantage builds on advantage.

## THE CONNECTION TO *KNOWN*

One of my editors read this chapter and said, "This sounds a lot like your book *KNOWN*." It does. A few years ago, I wrote a best-selling book with a step-by-step plan to build and launch your personal brand with this same slow-but-steady philosophy. And it works.

In a way, *Cumulative Advantage* is a companion book to *KNOWN*. I suppose it could even be considered KNOWN: Volume 2. Once you've built your brand, let's put some momentum behind it!

But the conclusion of both books is the same: You don't need the wealth, status, and Porcellian Club connections of a Winklevoss to become known or drive the momentum of Cumulative Advantage. You don't need to be famous or number one on Google to have amazing success.

All you require is the determination and grit to drive the steady progress of your own momentum.

I hope this energizes and inspires you. As long as you have a keyboard and a Wi-Fi connection, you can create. You can be heard. It doesn't matter who you are, where you're from, what you look like, how much money you have, or even how old you are. You can have a voice, you can find your audience, and you don't have to wait for somebody else to choose you.

You can choose yourself.

# REACHING OUT, REACHING UP

*"Surround yourself with people who
are going to take you higher."*

—OPRAH WINFREY

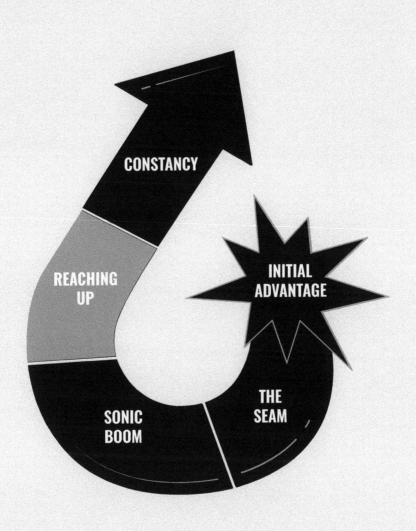

## CHAPTER 8

# REACHING OUT, REACHING UP

I want to take you on a voyage through space and time, to a fairer and more innocent place. Yes, we're going back to Chapter 1.

I explain in that scintillating chapter how the concept of Cumulative Advantage materialized from a surprising study of Nobel Laureates by Robert K. Merton and Harriet Zuckerman.

One unexpected discovery I didn't mention before was that of the 55 Nobel Laureates they studied, 46 of them (84 percent) had studied under a previous Nobel Prize winner! There was irrefutable evidence that these authoritative men (yes, they were all men) taught the next generation how to work the system and continue a legacy of influence and momentum. An intergenerational Matthew Effect!

Robert K. Merton efficiently used his lifetime of research to create his own Cumulative Advantage. Fittingly, his son, Robert C. Merton, a distinguished researcher and professor at MIT, won the 1997 Nobel Prize in economics.

This pattern provides an important clue about momentum for our own ideas and careers: It helps to have friends in high places who can lend a hand.

Think about the unexpected path of Robert K. Merton's own momentum. He was an impoverished first-generation immigrant who ultimately received a doctorate from Harvard and a place among the most famous sociologists in history.

Merton's hard work and keen intellect are undeniable. But we can't overlook the fact that he had some significant help along the way.

Merton began his academic career under the supervision of pioneering anthropologist George Eaton Simpson, the author of more than 60 books. Simpson arranged for Merton to receive an invitation to the prestigious American Sociological Association annual meeting where he befriended Pitirim Sorokin, the founding chair of the sociology department at Harvard University. Merton wrote, "I would not have dared apply for graduate study at Harvard had Sorokin not encouraged me to do so."[1]

This is a significant crossroads in the Merton success story. His career as a famous sociologist sprung from his Harvard experience. But in the 1930s, without the money and blue blood pedigree, it's unlikely he would have been accepted into Harvard without Sorokin lending a hand. During the

Depression when jobs were scarce, Sorokin secured a prized tutoring position for Merton at the university. He also named Merton as his research assistant, which led to the publication of Merton's first academic article in just his second year of study.

Merton said that Cumulative Advantage would work against us without a countervailing intervention. We can look to his own career for evidence.

Like Merton, I also believe it's possible to build momentum without the benefits of privilege. But if you haven't advanced from family wealth, connections, or education and reach the full boil of Cumulative Advantage on your own, you'll probably need a lift along the way.

You need a friend. Specifically, you need a friend with connections.

In this chapter, I'll take the idea of mentorship in a new direction. We'll learn to reach out and reach up.

## IT TAKES A VILLAGE

I didn't have to overcome life in the South Philadelphia slums like Robert Merton, but I spent my childhood stuffed into a tiny two-bedroom house with my five siblings in a modest blue-collar neighborhood. The nearest "playground" was a small grassy patch down the street next to a sewage plant that we called "Flushing Meadows."

I never went hungry ... except when Mom served tuna noodle casserole. No way. Couldn't handle that stuff. There was no money left after covering the essentials, so I learned from an early age that if I wanted something extra like a bicycle or a baseball bat, I'd have to earn the money myself. By the age of 10, I was raking leaves, washing cars, and selling packets of vegetable seeds door-to-door, not an easy pursuit in a close-packed neighborhood without a single garden!

My choice for a college education was thus simplified: With a combination of scholarships and working as many as three jobs at a time, West Virginia University was the only college I could afford.

I loved my WVU experience and the precious education I received there.

However, when it came to employment prospects, I was at a severe disadvantage. West Virginia is among the poorest states in America, and the nearest major employment center, Pittsburgh, was 80 miles away. The college was hard for corporate recruiters to get to, with just two or three flights a day arriving at the tiny Morgantown airport.

To connect to potential employers, I had to make something happen. I became the president of a student professional society and set about inviting guest speakers to campus from my favorite Pittsburgh companies. This provided a wonderful personal benefit. Everybody is flattered to speak at a university, and I was the one who spent two to three hours with my guests while they visited campus. In a not-so-subtle way, I was creating a dream team of new corporate connections.

One of the most-admired companies in our region was Alcoa. The company was founded in Pittsburgh in 1888 and still had its global headquarters in that beautiful river city. Alcoa was a Fortune 100 titan, a Dow Jones Industrial, and a company with a reputation for hiring the very best people. I created one of my speaker-connections at Alcoa, and when it was time to ask about a summer internship, my new friend replied, "Mark, you're really great but our internship is already filled. However, if you're ever in Pittsburgh, please stop by and see me."

I told him I would be in Pittsburgh the very next week (a big fat lie), and he invited me to lunch. I bought a suit, a tie, and an early-morning bus ticket to Pittsburgh. After spending a few hours with the Alcoa VP—including lunch at the Harvard-Yale-Princeton Club (a real thing)—he said to me, "I lied to you. We DO have an internship position open. But we only recruit at Ivy League Schools. We've never hired somebody from West Virginia, so I never considered you. I'm impressed that you came all the way to Pittsburgh to see me, and I'll give you a chance."

The very next week, I got back on that bus with the same suit and the same tie and went through a full day of interviews. I got the internship.

By the way, my only other internship offer was as a news reporter for the top-rated television station in Pittsburgh. If I had not forced open a door at Alcoa, you might be listening to me on the nightly news instead of reading this book!

The long-term implications of my proactive networking were profound. By taking the initiative to force myself into an opportunity, I overcame the disadvantage of the towering Ivy League walls that blocked me from a job at Alcoa.

After my internship, Alcoa hired me full-time. By the end of my career there, I was the company's global director of eCommerce and among the top 1 percent of its executives. I traveled the world, and Alcoa paid for me to attend graduate school and obtain two more degrees. Most important, I had connected with a lifetime of outstanding experts who supported me and guided me to the next opportunity.

As I interviewed people for this book, one theme stood out: To build Cumulative Advantage on your own, you need to reach out—and reach up.

## REINVENTING MENTORSHIP

Here's a definition of mentoring I found on a popular career site:

> Mentoring consists of a long-term relationship focused on supporting the growth and development of the mentee. The mentor becomes a source of wisdom, teaching, and support.

I think this definition is out of date for most people, especially a person like you who wants to build momentum.

If you need "wisdom and teaching" today, you don't need a long-term mentor. You need an internet connection.

The greatest value of mentoring that builds momentum is access. Access to opportunities. Access to insight. Access to people and scarce resources that can build momentum and lead to personal growth.

Information is useful, but it's a commodity normally available to anyone. Access is rare and drives unique momentum.

Now, if you're a tennis player, you'll need to get out on the court and learn from another tennis player. If you're a surgeon, I do not want you learning your craft from YouTube. Yes … in those cases your mentor needs to teach! But for most other professions today, it's time to reimagine the role of mentorship.

As an example, I'd like to share the story of Mellody Hobson, President and Co-CEO of Ariel Investments. Pick any area of professional life, and Mellody is a superstar. She's on the board of JPMorgan Chase and the Rockefeller Foundation. She's vice chair of Starbucks and was chairwoman of DreamWorks Animation. Mellody is a pioneering philanthropist who has started several important community organizations. In 2016, she was elected to the American Academy of Arts and Sciences.

But it all started with her initiative and the help of a mentor who opened new doors for her.[2]

"I came from difficult circumstances," she said. "Youngest of six kids, single mom, evicted a lot, phone disconnected, cars repossessed, government cheese, the whole thing. We heated our water on hot plates.

"Every single day, my mother told me, 'You can be anything.' I believed her, and because of those words, I would wake up at the crack of dawn excited to go to school and dream the biggest dreams.

"I was the first woman in my family to go to college, and I had a lot of work to do to figure things out. I met John Rogers, the founder of Ariel, when I was interviewing to be accepted to college, and I realized I could learn a lot from him. My sophomore year, I asked him if I could be a summer intern and he said yes.

"I would go in on Saturday mornings, sort the mail, and put it on his chair. One morning, I'm sitting in the reception area, sorting all this mail into piles and John walked in and said, 'What are you doing?' I said, 'I'm sorting the mail.' He said, 'Who told you to do that?' I said, 'No one, I just know you like information fast, so I'll just come here and sort the mail.'

"He sat down on the floor with me, and he started sorting the mail. Every Saturday after that, he came and sorted the mail with me.

"Then I got a full-time job working at Ariel. I knew that every Saturday morning, John went to this McDonald's on Wabash, in Chicago, to read. I started to show up—not in a bad stalker way—but to pay attention and to help organize the newspapers and magazines he likes to read. I didn't say anything. My whole thought is that if he wants to talk to me, he'll talk. But after a while he would say something. Week after week, month after month, he started to say more and more. Then he started giving me assignments. He wanted me to follow up on certain ideas.

"I wanted him to be a mentor to me, but I didn't ask him to do anything. I just made myself available in a way that was helpful. So now I'm 25 years old. John is taking me around the country to meet with people that he thinks I should know. He calls the CEO of Vanguard, whose name is Jack Bogle, who's on the board of Princeton. John said, 'I've got this young woman who went to Princeton, and I really want her to meet you.' Jack is like, 'Yeah ... great." He's not excited about it. John said, 'I really want her to meet you, you're an industry legend.' Jack said, 'I'm taking a train from New York to Philadelphia on this day, at this time, you can come and ride the train with me.'

"John and I flew to New York, landed at the airport, went to Penn Station, got on the train with him in the food car. We rode the train with Jack Bogle from New York to Philadelphia. On that train, John said this was an important connection for him because Mellody was going to be president of Ariel when she's 30. I was, like, 'What?' He said, 'I told my board, but they said that she has to wait until she's 30. You're a legend and I want her to be able to engage with you and ask you questions.'

"That is how John opened doors for me. John fundamentally helped me to be the person that I am. I cannot ever say enough good things about him.

"For me, obtaining those key experiences means going out and getting it, not ever waiting for it to come to you and not really not asking for the relationship."

# LUMPY MAIL

Mathew Sweezey is one of the most interesting people I've met in the last five years. Mathew is a marketing executive with Salesforce and the author of an important book, *The Context Marketing Revolution*. But one of his hidden talents is reaching out and reaching up for mentoring help. I'll let him tell his story:

"I was an agricultural business major in college—which is another whole story—and I took my first job selling copying machines on the south side of Atlanta. I hated life. It was literally the worst job I've ever had. Three months into the job I realized I had to get out and pursue my dream of getting into marketing. But I didn't have any direct experience on my resume. I had to come up with something to break out of this mold.

"I decided to learn marketing by marketing myself. I created this concept called lumpy mail, which is like three-dimensional direct mail.

"First, I identified all the CEOs of all the companies I wanted to work for. Then I created this package for them, which in hindsight was pretty cheesy. I took advantage of the fact that I had no experience and created this narrative that I was 'a seed for your organization—watch us grow together!' The package was quite big and elaborate with my own branding, seed packages, and soil. There were stickers on the outside of the box that said, 'Open promptly for freshness.' I think I put about $100 into each mailing. It was over the top.

"The logic was, I wanted to create a box that a CEO would actually open at their desk—something unlike anything they had ever seen. It was my only chance of breaking in because otherwise I had no experience. But I hoped to show enough initiative and creativity to get somebody's attention.

"I sent 10 of these boxes out, and half of the CEOs called me personally and responded. One CEO put a note on my package that said, "Hire this guy," and sent it to HR. That's how I got my first marketing job. Sight unseen.

"As I was becoming a marketing professional, I realized I needed to have mentors—I had a lot to learn. Just asking somebody to be your mentor is pretty lame. Instead, I created an entire curriculum of everything I wanted to learn from this person. I went online and studied all I could about a potential mentor. And then I created a lumpy mail just for them. I tried to put myself in their place and think, 'What questions would I like people to ask me?' and that became the heart of the curriculum.

"I tried to find mentors who are at the top of their field and the best in the world—so far past my reach—and the direct mail marketing has been the best way to connect with them.

"My last mentor was Peter Schwartz, the futurist who wrote *The Art of the Long View.* I've built relationships with amazing people in many different fields this way.

"My mentors have opened so many new doors for me. I've been introduced to key investors, new technology, and amazing thought leaders. The connection I had with Peter Schwartz led directly to me getting a promotion."

# HOW TO REACH OUT AND REACH UP

Of all the ideas I'm laying out to create your own Cumulative Advantage, I think that reaching out and reaching up to a mentor is the most important. The lessons and connections can be life-changing.

Here are some ideas on establishing a relationship with individuals who can help you build momentum:

## 1. Be clear

You can't find an ideal mentor until you can name your goals explicitly. If you can't describe where you want to go in life, how can somebody else help you get there? Your vision of your future will change over time ... and your mentors will, too.

Ragy Thomas of Sprinklr told me, "There is a Buddhist saying: 'When the student is ready, the teacher appears.' This means that when you're clear about the problem you're trying to solve, you also become very clear about the things you don't know that are needed to solve that problem. Most students don't find the right teachers because they're never ready. They don't have clarity about what they need to learn."

## 2. Study potential mentors

In a few days, you can usually learn enough about a person

from their digital footprint to understand their passions, strengths, and history. What was their career path? Key accomplishments? Have they written something, or have they been interviewed recently? If you don't learn everything you can about a potential mentor before approaching them, you'll look like an amateur.

You also need a sense of their values and the personal fit. I like observing a life through Instagram, where you can catch a glimpse of hobbies, family, and places that have meaning to a potential mentor. Is this somebody who could be a friend?

### 3. Develop a value proposition

"These thought leaders have a lot of people after them," Mathew Sweezey said. "But it's very rare when people reach out with a fully-formed plan and want to discuss theories and ideas with them. It's something that I enjoy, and they enjoy it, too. Most people want to consume their time. I want to add value."

Find connective tissue that can spark interest and add value to your mentor's life. Show them you did your homework.

### 4. Reach up

Don't just find someone who has a job you want. Find the type of person you aspire to be. That means getting clear on who you want to be.

Reach high. Mathew connected to one of the premier futurists of the world because he aspired to be in a similar position. Access to his world would be a great momentum-builder. Be persistent. If it doesn't work out with one person, try another.

Don't overlook your current relationships and the people who are already giving you advice. A mentor doesn't have to be older than you. They don't have to be in the same company or even work in the same field.

## 5. The Big Ask

Entrepreneur and author Ann Handley often says, "A big favor needs a big ask." How are you going to break through the clutter of this world to make a meaningful connection? It doesn't necessarily need to be "lumpy mail," but you need to find a way to build trust with a person and earn their attention in a way that promises some benefit.

A few pointers on the Big Ask:

- If possible, don't ask a person to be your mentor via email. Meeting face-to-face for coffee or a chat on the phone gives you a much better chance of making your case and addressing their concerns.
- Explain how much time and attention you'll need.
- Be ready to explain what you want to get out of the mentorship, why you want the person you're asking to be your mentor, and why you want a mentor in the first place.
- Explain that you're looking for access and opportunity, not a tutor.
- Suggest the value that is in it for the other person.

## 6. Let the relationship evolve organically

We often place unrealistic expectations on mentoring. We want to give it a name because it provides a sense of status and importance. But really, it's just a friendship. Mentoring is organic. It's healthy to let it grow like any other relationship—over time and based on mutual respect and trust.

Some business leaders advise avoiding the word "mentor" altogether. It can add pressure because it sounds too much like a formal commitment.

Instead try something like, "I really value your advice, would you be open to continuing the conversation?" Whatever you do, don't use the phrase "pick your brain." It immediately sounds like you want to use someone.

## 7. Gather a board of directors

At this point in my career, I don't have one mentor. I prefer to have a personal board of directors from diverse fields who I meet with on a regular basis (individually) to share ideas and solve problems. My "board" includes:

- An attorney who is also the founder of a software company
- An executive in the nonprofit industry
- The CEO of a Manhattan marketing agency
- An ex-IBM executive and company founder
- A consumer product researcher

These are trusted friends who will speak the truth and challenge me with their own thought-provoking ideas.

Another variation of this concept is the mastermind group. A mastermind group is typically led by a thought leader in a particular field who gathers like-minded individuals to share best practices and experiences. Sometimes you have to pay to join, but there are free groups that form, too.

Brooke Sellas, founder of B Squared Media, explained how it works for her: "My mastermind group is made up of five similar entrepreneurs who come together bimonthly to share ideas, thoughts, financials, feedback, contacts, and resources. Not only do we share our experience and 'Rolodex' of opportunities, but we also truly aim to advance each other's goals. This group has helped me navigate change in our industry and open new doors. There are no off-limit topics. The mastermind gives me a group of relevant peers who intelligently debate ongoing issues."

## 8. Go the extra mile

It's a busy, noisy world. Earning attention takes work. You don't necessarily have to create lumpy mail, but you'll probably have to do something special to earn these connections.

JaMarr Johnson had a distinguished career in both the United States Marines and the Navy. He was determined to make an impact on the business world and pursued a degree in accounting, but a chance opportunity to speak in front of a large crowd made him realize he was born to be an entertainer. In fact, he wanted to be a comedian.

You're probably thinking that it must be tough to move

from a career in the military and build momentum as an entertainer. That doesn't happen without some help.

JaMarr settled in San Francisco and was always looking for a break to get on stage. "My superpower is connecting with people," he said. "And I'm never afraid to ask for an opportunity. I met a woman who was a sales director with Eventbrite, and the company was sponsoring events around the city called 'Moonlighting SF'—a monthly variety show. I wanted to get on this show, so I came to one of her events and brought a bunch of paying customers with me. I wanted to show her that not only could I perform, I could also market the event for her. That impressed her, and she said she would try to get me on the stage in a couple of months.

"Two months later I had an email from her, 'Hey, come on the show.' I go to the show and I kill it. They loved me!

"A month later, she tells me that her show host backed out—could I be the host? I had never done anything like that before, but I said 'Sure,' and I kill it again. Next thing I know, she makes me the full-time host.

"She then selected me to be the mainstage coordinator at the 2015 Pride Festival. Now I'm performing in front of 20,000 people. And I killed it. Then I'm being invited to host Oscar parties and some of my best-paying gigs ever, and my career just kept rolling. And every time I perform, it helps me make new connections for my marketing business, too.

"Once I had the door open for me, my career spiraled forward."

# THE TIM FERRISS GUIDE TO CONNECTING

I already mentioned how I created a team of mentors early in my career and a "board of directors" later in my career. There is no way I would have the momentum I have today without their help.

Let's check in with Team Ferriss.

In an interview about the importance of mentorship, Tim revealed his secret process for building connections.[3] It might sound familiar!

"One of the best ways to develop relationships with experienced people is through volunteering. In 1999, I had no money and no resources. I knew nobody. But I drove to Silicon Valley in my beat-up green car, and it was such an exciting time because I was full of hope.

"I volunteered at a number of events like the Silicon Valley Association of Startup Entrepreneurs. There are many, many events like this that attract business leaders, and they exist everywhere. I volunteered to fill water glasses, hand out tickets, and anything else that was needed as a way to meet people.

"I realized quickly that you don't have to do very much as a volunteer to stand out! Most people who volunteer do just the bare minimum.

"I found that by doing extra things I got the attention of the organizers, and within a few months they were inviting me to plan meetings that would be attended by more than 500 people. I decided on the theme and the speakers. And that gave me the chance to reach out to all of these people I selfishly wanted to get to know, including Jack Canfield, the author of the *Chicken Soup for the Soul* series of books; Gary Erickson, who revolutionized sports nutrition as creator of the Clif Bar; and Trip Hawkins, who is co-founder of Electronic Arts.

"I got to know all of them. And the more I pitched people to attend the event, the better I got. Now, a key point—I did not ask them to be my mentors. But every six months when I genuinely had a life question that one of my contacts could help with, I sent them a short email to keep the connection going. I built these important friendships by playing the long game.

"Seven years later, Jack Canfield was the one who introduced me to the person who became my book agent. The entire venture of what became *The 4-Hour Workweek* never would have happened had it not been for Jack.

"Anybody can meet people like that. You just have to swallow your pride and focus on learning first and never making the relationship transactional. You don't have to 'network.' You just have to be a good human being."

# THE LIFT

When I started working on this book, I couldn't have dreamed that Tim Ferriss and I employed a similar strategy to attract mentors in high places. But I think this is something more than an extraordinary coincidence.

Without question, reaching out and reaching up is a critical part of building momentum. You can't sit around and wait for it to happen. Today, there's a lot of buy-in to a "hustle culture" that glorifies impossibly long hours of work. What's lacking from that equation is initiative. Neither Tim nor I hustled our way into inner circles, but we did create positive action through initiative.

Nurturing meaningful relationships with people who can help and guide you takes persistence and practice, but there is probably nothing more important when it comes to creating momentum.

We're nearing the end of the book, and it's time for the big reveal. Up until this point, it still seems like both Tim and I had an equal chance to reach Oprah Orbit. Now you're about to find out why he did and I didn't.

# CONSTANCY OF PURPOSE

*"Getting an audience is hard. Sustaining an audience is hard. It demands a consistency of thought, of purpose and of action over a long period of time."*

—BRUCE SPRINGSTEEN

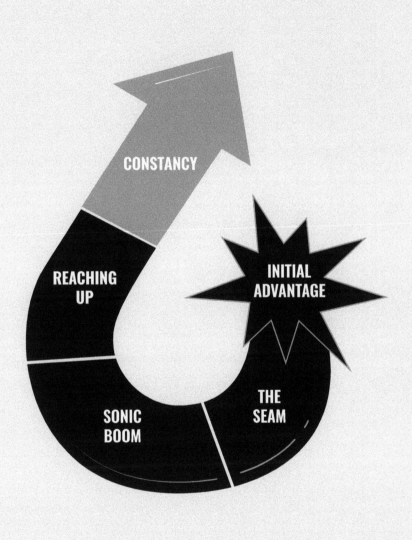

# CHAPTER 9

# CONSTANCY OF PURPOSE

The Matthew Effect shows that initial advantage can originate from almost anything. It could be access to resources, a powerful friend who can help you, or an even idea in your head.

It could even be sugar, salt, and smoke.

Allow me to explain.

Allan Benton operates a pint-sized store in Madisonville, Tennessee, just a short drive from my home. If you're motoring down Highway 411, you'll have to look hard for it or you'll pass the 1980s vintage storefront. The cluttered interior is even less impressive. Allan still answers a rotary dial telephone to talk to customers.

But what happens in the smoky rooms just behind the humble storefront is magic.

Allan Benton makes the best bacon in the world.

If you're reading this book in a country where you've never experienced the miracle of American bacon, you won't fully appreciate this story. I've been to 72 different countries and had bacon in most of them … at least, they call it bacon.

American bacon is entirely different. It's a thick and juicy art form on par with jazz and basketball as one of my country's most beautiful gifts to the world.

Bacon is also a commodity. Americans eat so much bacon (an average of 18 pounds a year) that the processing has been thoroughly automated and industrialized on a colossal scale.

But not in this beat-up little store in the middle of nowhere. Every pound of Benton's bacon is cured by hand over a month. And it has become world famous.

Here's how Allan found his initial advantage, in his own words.[1]

"I was born in Scott County, Virginia, so far back in the hills that you had to look straight up to see daylight. We couldn't go to the grocery store and buy meats of any kind. We raised everything we ate, and we had to preserve this meat so it would be available without refrigeration all year long.

"We lived on that cured pork and counted on it to sustain us. I started curing meats as a business with this same process used in my family for generations.

"My original family recipe was two parts salt, one part brown sugar, and a handful of red and black pepper. You rub it on a slab by hand. This mixture starts a drying process that takes the moisture out of the ham, removing the environment where bacteria can survive so that it will keep without refrigeration."

Benton's bacon is not for the faint of heart. After being cured in that mixture for 10 days, it's aged for another 10 before spending three days in a hickory smoke-filled room. What emerges is intensely smoky bacon, dusty reddish-brown and with a perfume that will make your house smell like an Appalachian campfire.

While it takes a month for Mr. Benton to prepare his bacon, big packing houses push their product out the door in 24 hours. "We process about 40,000 bacon bellies per year ... the bigger packers will do that much in a day," he said. "One day for them equals our yearly production!"

Now, here comes the best lesson from Mr. Benton:

"I had been in business for five years and I told my dad, 'I'm not going to make it. I'm going to have to quick-cure our meats because I simply can't compete with these big competitors. They're selling them fully processed for the same prices that I'm BUYING the meat!'

"And my dad told me, 'Son, if you play the other fella's game, you will always lose. Stick with your focus on quality. Quality makes you different. Quality will always win in the end.'"

Allan's initial advantage that led to his momentum was a decidedly low-tech process of hand-rubbing, hand-curing, and hand-smoking meat in a way that made it unique. Through a common-sense business analysis, he saw that his business was vulnerable, and he almost lost sight of his only real point of differentiation. Gratefully, he listened to his father.

Eventually, Allan's superior product attracted the attention of the famed chef John Fleer from the exclusive Blackberry Farm resort near Knoxville, Tennessee.

As other notable chefs came to visit Fleer's kitchen, he introduced them to this remarkable ingredient, and soon Benton's brand was featured in some of the top restaurants in the world.

But Mr. Benton almost blew it. Without his father's advice, he might have trudged down a path of automation that would have made him the same as everybody else and ruined his business.

Author Jim Collins of *Good to Great* fame calls this tendency the "doom loop." When a company faces a crisis, it reacts without discipline, grasping at any fad or new direction, only to experience more disappointment.

This is an exceptionally important lesson. To achieve the momentum of Cumulative Advantage, you need to recognize your initial point of differentiation, and you also have to *stick with it*.

Achieving the full force of Cumulative Advantage requires constancy of purpose.

# A SERIES OF SMART DECISIONS

No matter your goal, committing to constancy of purpose might mean years or even a lifetime of consistent effort.

Recognizing small advantages—those doors of opportunity—can happen for anybody. But the Cumulative Advantage only occurs when a person decides to overcome obstacles and do something about them.

In this book I've used a simple graphic to illustrate the path toward Cumulative Advantage. But a more accurate representation would be a long line of these swooshing arrows. New doors of initial advantage are probably opening all the time. A life is a continuous timeline of opportunities to consider. How do you know whether to stick with your idea, as Mr. Benton did, or open a new door?

Once you've established momentum, you need to sustain it through a series of smart decisions, and the first one is to determine if you're heading in the right direction. You burst through a seam but rarely know the full extent of the opportunity until the momentum begins. To determine if your momentum is actually leading to your goals, you'll need to answer two questions:[2]

## 1. Is your momentum relevant?

It's time to reflect on the alignment with your overall goal. Are you trying to start a business or grow one? Are you trying to spread an idea or write a book? Do you want to build momentum for a career? Is the momentum pushing you in the right direction?

Check for relevance. Once you've entered the seam, does your audience or customer base *care* about your idea? Are they willing to pay you, or listen to you? Is the audience or customer base big enough to matter? Is the effort required to sustain your momentum aligned with the size of the opportunity?

The relevance of your momentum is LOW and it's time for a shift if

- Your core audience wants more for less.
- Their purchase frequency or attention is declining.
- Customers are seeking new capabilities well outside your core competency.
- You'll require more resources just to maintain the status quo.

The relevance of your momentum is HIGH and it's time to double-down on your efforts if

- What you're offering is highly valued and demanded by an expanding, accessible audience.
- The returns on incremental investments in time and capabilities are strong and growing.
- There are high barriers to entry, meaning that your momentum is putting you out of reach of competitors.

## 2. Can your Cumulative Advantage be sustained?

Does your current direction deliver meaningful differentiation? Does it have a difference that makes a difference?

Check for sustainability. How durable is that advantage? Can you stay on this path and be successful for a long time, or will competitors eventually burst through the same seam and overwhelm you?

The sustainability of your momentum is LOW and it's time for a shift if

- Others can replicate, improve upon, or offer a viable substitute for what you do.
- Customers view you as undifferentiated.
- You're becoming distracted or bored. If you don't love what you're doing, you'll probably quit.

The sustainability of your momentum is HIGH and it's time to double-down on your momentum if

- Few competitors can deliver and sustain what you do well.
- Customers view you as highly differentiated.
- Your passion, commitment, and enthusiasm are high.

# MAKING CHOICES THAT BUILD MOMENTUM

Whether you're building momentum for an idea, a career, a social cause, or a business, there are universal factors that can help fuel that turbine.

If the momentum is relevant, meaningful, sustainable, and directionally correct, it's time to put your foot on the gas pedal.

## 1. Set powerful goals

An old business adage is "measure what you treasure." The most important benefit of setting goals isn't achieving your goal. It's how you organize your life or company to achieve your goal that's the real benefit. The goal creates the activity. The goal can change a life, or a company, or a country.

In my corporate days, my company would set "quantum leap" goals. When you first heard about a new goal, the initial reaction was usually, "No way. That seems impossible." But amazing things can happen when you provide laser-focus to a dream. And achieving a stretch goal like this creates an entire culture of enthusiasm and momentum.

## 2. Adopt an environment that supports the goal

Achieving a quantum leap goal cannot depend on willpower alone. Willpower is the slowest and most ineffective way to drive momentum because it's focused on incremental and linear growth, usually based on past performance.

When you commit to a goal that far exceeds your current capability, you'll need a new environment that organically supports your goal—a context that *forces* you to become more than you currently are. Once you design the right conditions, your desired behavior naturally flows forward.

If you want to become a world-class cyclist or make a leap from an office job to starting your own business, your entire environment will need to support that goal. Dr. Bruce Lipton says in his book, *The Biology of Belief*, "Just like a single cell, the character of our lives is determined not by our genes but by our responses to the environmental signals that propel life."

A small example from my own career: Simply choosing what room I work in dramatically affects my productivity. I can't completely understand it, but a combination of environmental stimulation (or lack of it), ambience, surrounding colors, the comfort of a certain chair ... it all goes into a productivity cocktail. I've written most of my books from one overstuffed chair in my bedroom.

Consciously designing your environment with the best resources is like creating a river that runs directly toward your goal.

## 3. Change your role in the narrative

In the course of my research for this book, I came across fascinating studies that demonstrate how humans live up to a narrative that is created about them over time.[3]

Your life becomes a self-fulfilling prophecy and you may not even know it. Changing your narrative can change your life!

That life narrative might come from your role in a relationship, your position within an organization, and even childhood events that lock you in a place in a certain story. These made-up roles and expectations can be self-limiting when it comes to developing momentum for your life and career.

This issue came up in an individual coaching session when a friend said she dreamed of writing a book but felt this was impossible since she had been humiliated by failing English twice in high school. She has put herself in a place where a dream cannot be realized because of some historical narrative.

Changing her narrative would be: "I have lots of great ideas and an amazing story to tell. My goal is to write a book, and I will change my environment to support that, including prioritizing my time, learning the book writing process, using technology that can improve my writing, and finding the editing help that I need. Besides, my high school English teacher was a jerk!"

As I've been writing this book, it's been eye-opening to reconsider the place I hold in the narratives of my family, my marriage, and even among my clients and social media audience.

Sometimes a role I've historically played led to esteem from others ... but this role might not be useful or even accurate anymore. Part of my narrative comes from being the oldest of six children. I was held in a place of responsibility and served as a backup parent for most of my teen years. I still have a lot of that narrative running in my life today, for better or for worse.

I don't want any of my paths to progress to be blocked because of what people think I should or shouldn't do. The good news is, I'm still discovering new opportunities for myself, even after all these decades in the business world.

You and I have a choice to either conform to that prescribed narrative or redefine how we view ourselves based on what is really true. Can you see the narratives that constrain you?

## 4. Lifeline relationships

I spent the last chapter explaining the importance of getting a momentum boost from mentors who create new opportunities for you.

But these relationships are also crucial to sustaining momentum for the long-term. In the book, *Who's Got Your Back*, Keith Ferrazzi dispels the myth of the lone professional "superhero" and our culture's go-it-alone mentality.

According to Ferrazzi, the real path to success in work and life is through creating an inner circle of *lifeline relationships*. These are deep, close relationships with a few trusted individuals who will offer the encouragement, feedback, and generous mutual support you need to reach your full potential.

These lifeline relationships are the people who make sure you don't give up and quit. If you're pursuing a true quantum leap goal, you'll undoubtedly find yourself in a situation where you need support. These friends can also help hold you accountable to your goals.

## 5. Discipline sustains momentum

Nick Saban is famous for "the process," his organization-wide focus on discipline that helped him become one of the most successful American football coaches in history. He described how discipline is connected to positive momentum:[4]

"There's probably one really memorable game that changed the psychological approach we use to motivate teams, and it happened when we played Ohio State in 1998.

"Ohio State had been ranked number one all season. We were 4-5 and not a very good team, but we won that game because leading up to the game we decided to not focus on the outcome. We were just going to focus on the process of what it took to play the best football we could play—focus on each particular play as if it had a history and life of its own.

"I told my players not to look at the scoreboard, don't look at any external factors. All your focus and concentration, all your effort, all your toughness, all your discipline goes into executing the next play. Regardless of what happened—success or failure—you move on to the next play with the same focus, and you do that for an entire game. If you have that discipline, you can live with the results regardless of what those results are."

"I'm convinced that the process-oriented approach is valuable because it provides the discipline to focus on the right things—not the results, but whatever is in your control to achieve those results.

"There are two pains in life. The pain of discipline and the pain of disappointment. If you can handle the pain of discipline, you'll never have to deal with the pain of disappointment."

Successful people choose healthy and productive habits over a stagnant life. Momentum requires discipline. For you, "the process" might look like making sales calls every hour, writing your book every day, or reaching up for entrepreneurial guidance every month.

There is no growth without momentum. There is no momentum without discipline.

## 6. Resilience

In my original survey research for this book, successful entrepreneurs acknowledged that initial advantage, promotion, and mentors helped create momentum. But there was another common theme critical to constancy of purpose: tenacity. Here's a typical quote from the anonymized data:

"What helped me build momentum is my determination, persistence, and work ethic. You get knocked back so often as an entrepreneur and you need to keep going. You need to be the type that just keeps working without the need for someone to push you along."

"The idea of the founder story and the aha moment is tremendously overrated," Ragy Thomas of Sprinklr told me. "Sure, these random moments occur. There are probably 17 million moments like that in a lifetime. But it doesn't mean anything without conviction. Speaking as an entrepreneur without a lot of early advantages, you must have the right idea combined with the right mindset, the right skillset, the right market opportunity—and then fight to make it come alive. When you begin to launch an idea, it will be dying every second unless you keep it alive. Conviction wins the war."

In her seminal book *Grit*,[5] Angela Duckworth describes the four core personality traits of people with the exceptional persistence needed to create momentum over time:

- **Love of the work:** Success begins with enjoying what you do. Every gritty person Angela studied for her book can point to aspects of their work they enjoy less than others, and most have to put up with chores they don't enjoy at all. Nevertheless, they're captivated by the endeavor as a whole. With enduring fascination and childlike curiosity, they practically shout, "I love what I do!"

- **Forward progress:** After defining your open seam, you must devote yourself to the focused, full-hearted, challenge-exceeding practice that leads to momentum. Zero in on your weaknesses and commit to improving, week after month after year. To be gritty is to resist complacency. "Whatever it takes, I want to improve!" is a refrain of all paragons of grit, no matter their particular interest or how excellent they already are.

- **Purpose:** For most people, work without purpose is nearly impossible to sustain for a lifetime. Gritty people are driven because they can say, "My work is important—both to me and to others."

- **Hope:** Hope is a rising-to-the-occasion kind of perseverance. From the very beginning to the very end, it's important to keep going even when things are difficult, even when you have doubts. At various points, in big ways and small, you get knocked down. If you stay down, grit loses. If you get up, grit prevails.

When people fail to execute on an opportunity, it's probably due to some deficit in one of these characteristics. If you find any of the following thoughts going through your head, you're probably at the end of the trail:

- "I'm bored."
- "The effort isn't worth it."
- "This isn't important to me."
- "I can't do this, so I might as well give up."

There's nothing wrong with having thoughts like these. But if one of these statements is the story in your head right now, it's time to pivot and try another path.

An insurmountable roadblock is not the same as a downfall. It's a chance to take control. Honestly addressing the issues in an ego-free manner will help you avoid years of frustration and move you on a more fruitful journey. A roadblock is a reminder that we have more growing to do and new parts of ourselves to discover.

## 7. Be Brené

I will never be a professional basketball player because I'm too old and I have bad knees. There are certain limitations beyond our control. But I don't think courage is one of them.

When we're born, we have this precious clean slate of a personality. I have never seen a toddler who was not courageous, whether they're taking a first step or trying to taste a handful of dirt. And then through the years, good and bad things happen that forge our adult personality, and I think for many people, courage is just pounded right out of us.

*If only I had the courage*, we often say to ourselves, as though courage is something only a lucky few possess. But that's not true. Within you lies all the courage you will ever need to make that change or take that chance in your work, relationships, and life.

If you've followed me through my blog or podcast, you'll undoubtedly know that one of my all-time heroes is researcher and author Brené Brown. I want to be the Boy Brené when I grow up.

If you're afraid to do what it takes to build momentum, the best advice I can offer is to read her book *Dare to Lead*. Brené is the Queen of Brave, and she can help you identify the obstacles blocking your inherent courage.

## 8. Start over if you need to

It takes courage to begin. It also takes courage to end.

There have been plenty of examples in this book where the timing wasn't right and an idea had to end. It's scary and heartbreaking to come to a full stop, but dramatic restarts can also be new beginnings.

When I started my first business, I made money, but I found that I didn't like the work as much as I thought I would. I had found my seam, but it didn't align with my values. I had to make a hard pivot. That was disappointing and a little scary, but it led to much bigger opportunities and a much happier Mark.

And it's also the reason why I don't know Oprah.

# THE FINAL ROUND

We now come to the point of the big reveal and answer the question I posed more than 100 pages ago: Why does Tim Ferriss know Oprah and I don't?

Up until this point in our Expedition to Oprah, the two of us were tracking in lockstep and building momentum that could lead to Cumulative Advantage.

- We both had a small initial advantage, a click moment based on some random event in our lives.
- The timing of our work seemed right, although Tim had the advantage of a world looking for a guru.
- We both acted on our insights and set our Cumulative Advantage in motion by creating a "sonic boom."

- By reaching out and reaching up, we had a cadre of mentors who helped create new opportunities and propel us forward.

The next, and final, challenge was to capitalize on our success, leverage our newfound Cumulative Advantage, and fuel the momentum even further. Like Mr. Benton, it was time to make some bacon.

Tim did a superb job elevating his momentum through his constancy of purpose and precise execution. He created another sonic boom when he blew up on the speaking circuit, appearing on some of the biggest stages in the world like TED, SXSW, and LeWeb. His speaking fees soared.

As a *New York Times* best-selling author, he had access to new mentors to help propel him into the next level of celebrity orbit. He earned the attention of Mike Maples, who taught him the insider secrets of investing as a venture capitalist. He used this knowledge to invest in StumbleUpon, Posterous, Evernote, Shopify, Uber, and TaskRabbit, to name a few.

And he turned the "4-Hour" book idea into a franchise, following his success with *The 4-Hour Chef* and the controversial *4-Hour Body*, both New York Times best sellers.

On a whim, Tim started a podcast, and it vaulted to the top of the charts on iTunes, attracting lucrative sponsors eager to connect to his millions of fans.

And of course, he was invited to contribute to Oprah Winfrey's blog.

Me? Here's the real reason I never attained Oprah Orbit: I chose not to. It didn't fit with my life plan.

While Tim stuck to his constancy of purpose and generated a "4-Hour" craze, I stopped in my tracks and started working on new, unrelated projects.

I looked at writing *Return On Influence* as an adventure in intellectual curiosity. If I was to spend a year of my life writing a book, it had better be interesting—and the emerging opportunity of influence marketing was fascinating to me!

When the momentum surged and my star began to rise, I realized I had an undefended opportunity to become an authority in influence marketing. I could have leveraged my research and new connections to start a pioneering influencer marketing agency or consulting practice. I could have used my progress to create Cumulative Advantage, just like Tim.

But I had zero interest in this.

The momentum was misaligned with my ikigai. My drive and personal energy comes from trying new things. I have a history of reinventing myself about every three to four years, so the idea of committing to the path of one topic seemed depressing to me. And the stress of starting an agency? Just the thought of it makes me ill! In a way, not following through on an obvious opportunity was a way to take command of my own narrative.

So, I terminated the momentum and waited for others to step into the seam and drive my ideas forward. And they did! Almost every sizable advertising and marketing agency in the country now has some sort of influence marketing component.

One of the proudest moments of my career came when I received this note from a young man named Zak Stahlsmith:

> I just wanted you to know how much your book has meant to me. When I read Return On Influence, it changed my life. I knew this is what I wanted to do, and I started an agency focused on influence marketing. Because of you, I have a successful and growing business in my hometown in Pennsylvania and I'm able to provide many good-paying jobs for my community. Thank you.

So … it worked out.

I don't know Oprah, but I'm living a happy, rewarding life that provided at least one spark for another person who is able to care for his family and employees because of me.

That's all I need. And maybe some Benton's bacon.

Oh yes … Oprah, I know you're probably reading this. I'm still out here.

Ready when you are.

# CHAPTER 10

# AFTERWORD

In my books, I let facts and research tell the story, and I try to present them in an entertaining fashion. But as I bring these ideas to you, I'm learning a lot along the way, too. For me, publishing a book takes two years of intense reading, studying, writing, and rewriting. It's like earning a master's degree in something new each time I embark on a project.

In this final chapter, I'll do something I've never done before in my books. Instead of just writing from my brain, I want to write from my conscience, too.

In a way, I'm taking my own medicine. I'm challenging the narrative about what people think I should or shouldn't say because the research and writing of this book has been a humbling, profound, and emotional journey that has haunted me. I would be a coward to not say what has to be said.

This experience has made me feel like my eyeglasses have a new prescription for a Matthew Effect lens. I now observe parenting, business opportunities, career choices, and current events through the new clarity of this lens.

For example, when a new friend tells me their life story, I listen carefully to detect a possible early-life initial advantage, the momentum that grew with the help of mentors, and the decisions that came next to keep the turbine going. This is a pattern that repeats endlessly, and now that you've read this book, I think you'll see it, too.

But the most impactful change on me is how I view history and our future through the lens of Cumulative Advantage.

## THE STREETS WERE BURNING

Perhaps the dimension of initial advantage that transcends all others is to be born into a safe home, with two parents, in a prosperous, developed country ... as I was.

I grew up in the great and beautiful river city of Pittsburgh, Pennsylvania. Although the 1960s of my childhood was a cataclysmic period of civil discord, I was oblivious. My obsession was baseball, and posters of beloved Black men adorned my bedroom walls and those of most of my friends.

My greatest hero was baseball slugger Willie Stargell, a gifted athlete, charismatic captain of two World Series championship teams, and a big-hearted community leader whose autographed photo still hangs in my office. I joined other Pittsburghers in cheering the accomplishments of sports heroes of color such as Roberto Clemente, Franco Harris, Lynn Swann, and of course "Mean" Joe Greene.

I now know that all of these men I loved so much were more than star athletes. They were also civil rights leaders in their own way ... because they had to be. Just 20 years before, Black men weren't even allowed to step foot on a professional baseball field. They confronted racism in some form every day. But I had no sense of history or context when I was 8 years old. I couldn't comprehend the daily personal challenges my heroes must have faced.[1]

One of my earliest childhood memories is watching the evening TV news reports after the assassination of Martin Luther King Jr. in 1968. The streets were burning in many American cities. It was frightening because I couldn't understand the violent turmoil. I had nightmares about these images. I remember trying to read a newspaper to understand what was happening, but the words were too confusing for a third grader. It felt like I was entering Act 2 of a play and I couldn't understand the plot because I missed the explanation at the beginning.

As a child, I expected an orderly solution to whatever this was about. If we had problems in America, we would overcome them like they taught us in school. We would take care of each other just like we did in my family and in my neighborhood when people needed help.

Dr. King condemned rioting but said a riot is the "language of the unheard." I'm peering into the final third of my life and—*50 years later*—the streets are still burning. I wonder ... will they still be burning 50 years from now? How do we end the cycle?

## CUMULATIVE DISADVANTAGE

For more than a decade, I've mentored economically disadvantaged children. They have become my extended family. A map of violent crime in our city would show these kids live near the epicenter of our city's problem areas. If you follow me on social media, you've probably seen me with these children, especially a young man named Elijah who I've tried to support and mentor since he was 7 years old.

This is a particularly tricky part of my narrative. When providing self-disclosure like this, I run the risk of coming across as "Hey! Look at me and my good works!" I ask you to oblige me with grace as I tell a personal story to make an important point.

When Elijah was 10 years old, I took him on a camping trip to a favorite state park. I had just come back from a big tech conference where I had seen a vast ballroom of children his age hunched over computers writing code for their robots. I was overwhelmed with emotion as I observed this opportunity gap. The kids I cared for had no idea this world of pint-sized coders existed! I guessed they couldn't *imagine* how far behind they were. Many of the kids I worked with didn't have personal computers or Wi-Fi at that time, let alone kits to make personal robots.

On our drive to the camping trip, this bright little boy turned to me and said, "I am so happy to be with you today. If I had stayed at home, I'd have to go to my cousin's funeral. He was stabbed 22 times and was even stabbed in the eye. I did not want to see that."

That is not a conversation anyone should be having with a 10-year-old.

A few years later, I was in Europe and saw a news alert on my phone that there was an active shooter on Elijah's street. I called him immediately. When he heard the shots, he told me that he ran as fast as he could and hid behind the shelves in a nearby store. A few months later, he was playing in front of the home of Zaevion Dobson, his close friend. Just hours later that same day, Zaevion died in that front yard while shielding three girls from a gang-related shooting spree, a heroic act that made the national news.

Elijah, who is Black, and six other children have been raised by his saintly grandmother. A rock of a woman. His mother was in a penitentiary for several years. There are no active fathers around. There is almost no child support for any of these children. Their house is always clean, the children are always fed and at school on time, but there's not a lot of room for many "extras" in this family that I love.

For example, for Christmas one year, Elijah told me he wanted a door. He was sleeping in a ground-floor room, and the television noise at night prevented him from sleeping well. So I worked with his grandmother to hang a door in the house.

Even after seeing the undertow pulling at these children for more than 12 years, I'm not discouraged. Elijah comes from a family of boundless hope and love. It is a family with countervailing processes, and I will come back to that in a moment.

## SURFING YOUR WAVE

The Matthew Effect and the widening gap between haves and have-nots is not exactly a common topic of dinnertime conversation. When I first started discussing the ideas for this book, people would get this far-off look on their face and say, "Hmmm ... now that I think about it, I can see that I'm in this place in my life due to the circumstances of certain advantages and events. I hadn't thought about it that way before. Where would I be if I didn't have that luck along the way? That person to pull me along when I needed it?"

For me, that far-off look is reassuring. That look means they're viewing their lives in a new way—as surfers riding the crests of waves that started long ago. Some people ride towering Winklevoss waves, some people ride blue-collar waves, and some people are getting dragged down beneath their waves in a deadly undertow.

Being white, rich, or college-educated is certainly not a certified "golden ticket" for life. Hard work and talent matter. Even the Winklevoss twins had to make smart decisions and not blow their money on bad choices. Every living human being has their struggles, pain, and barriers in life. "To live is to suffer," Viktor Frankl writes in *Man's Search for Meaning*.

But to some degree, the Matthew Effect amplifies everyone's prior advantages and disadvantages. As Malcolm Gladwell said, both the fortunes of the fortunate and the misfortunes of the unfortunate are in some way unearned and undeserved.

On some level I've always known this, but I haven't always *expressed* it. Self-interest, individualism, and personal pride are powerful forces. Telling people the heroic tale of how I fought my way into my first job with Alcoa (Chapter 8) seems a lot more natural than explaining that every person who interviewed me for the job was a white male, every boss I had in my 27-year corporate career was a white male, all but one professor over four years of MBA studies was a white male, every person who has hired me for a professional speaking gig in the past 10 years has been white, and ... well, you get the point.

I've never felt that I don't belong in a personal or professional environment due to my race, with the possible exception of the time I was lost in the Tokyo subway system, but that's a story for another day.

A major benefit of being white in America is simply feeling like you belong. As my career progressed, I never had to deal with a coworker's resentment that I only got the job because I'm white. I am assumed to be the most qualified candidate. Nobody refers to me as "an important white writer."

It's hard to not be protective of my "pulled up from the bootstraps" narrative. I overcame many obstacles. I took huge risks. And I'm proud of what I accomplished. But I also realize it's a lot easier surfing a towering wave in corporate

America when almost everyone in your circle has surfed the same wave.

# THE TYRANNY OF MERIT

In America and much of the world, it is an article of faith that if we provide a truly level playing field, everyone has an equal chance. And if everything is equal, those who rise by the sweat of their effort, talent, and hard work have earned their place in society. This is the American Dream.

In his book *The Tyranny of Merit*, political philosopher Michael Sandel lays out two fundamental objections to this cherished ideal.[2] First, and most obvious, the fabled "level playing field" doesn't exist for a large part of the population. He notes that his own Harvard students are convinced their success is a result of their own effort, but two-thirds of them come from the top 20 percent of the income scale.

The relationship between social class and SAT scores (which grade high school students ahead of college) is well-documented, and the situation is not improving.[3]

Research shows that a whopping 60 percent of the variance in IQ is attributable to socioeconomic status, home environment, and nutrition. Children aged 4 to 6 living in poor conditions who were adopted into enriched living conditions experienced an average IQ increase from 77 to 91[4].

Sandel notes that social mobility has also been stalled for decades. "Americans born to poor parents tend to stay poor as adults."

According to *The Wall Street Journal*, differences in income and wealth have barely changed in the 50 years since I saw those frightening images on TV.

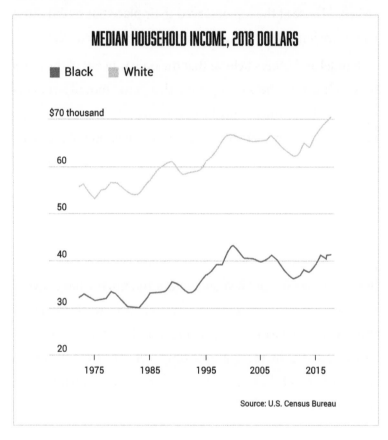

MEDIAN HOUSEHOLD INCOME, 2018 DOLLARS

■ Black ■ White

*Source: U.S. Census Bureau*

While all racial groups saw their wealth devastated by the 2008 financial crisis, Black wealth has been much slower to recover. In recent years, the median Black household had $18,000 in net worth compared with $171,000 for whites.[5]

But the main point of *The Tyranny of Merit* is that this ubiquitous adoration of the "self-made success" creates an unfair and humiliating status for those who don't have the same early-life advantages. "The implication is that those who do not rise will have no one to blame but themselves," Sandel writes. "Those at the top deserved their place but so did those who were left behind. They hadn't striven as effectively."

Sandel and others believe that the only way out of the crisis is to reimagine the assumptions that have morally rubber-stamped the winners and losers in society. The COVID-19 pandemic, and in particular the new appreciation of the value of supposedly unskilled, low-paid work, offers a starting point for renewal.

"This is a moment to begin a debate about the dignity of work," he writes, "about the rewards of work both in terms of pay but also in terms of esteem. We now realize how deeply dependent we are, not just on doctors and nurses, but delivery workers, grocery store clerks, warehouse workers, truck drivers, home healthcare providers and childcare workers, many of them in the gig economy. We call them essential workers and yet these are oftentimes not the best paid or the most honored workers."

## HOPE, ESTEEM, AND OUR CHILDREN

This idea of redistributing esteem became a theme as I researched this book. My friend Wendy Laman has been an early childhood educator, consultant, and administrator for more than 30 years, with much of that time spent serving children living in impoverished, crime-ridden neighborhoods. She has been immersed in the Matthew Effect mire of inequality for most of her life.

Here's what I wanted to know: After this long career and relentless challenges, does she have hope? Can the Matthew Effect gaps ever close?

"I do have hope," Wendy said. "The big changes that have to happen in society aren't necessarily tied just to government programs trying to fix economic problems. I see real change begin to happen when a child hears that they are valued and important and they truly believe it to be so. That is the game-changer ... but this belief must be nourished, supported, and reinforced to sustain long-term growth and meaningful change."

Gloria Nolan, a community leader fighting for early education resources in poor neighborhoods of St. Louis, agrees. In her city, school funding depends on revenue from local property taxes. "If you look at our area," she said, "progress is just not going to happen without an intervention. Our hope to reverse these trends is in our children. But their self-esteem and confidence has to be nurtured through a system of supportive resources. I don't think the government is going to be able to reverse the trend. It's up to us. The people have to do the work."

I want to emphasize that I'm not pinning the hopes of an entire generation on the redistribution of esteem. The root causes of inequity and injustice are cosmically complex. Where do you even start?

For months, I agonized over the proper way to end this book. The gap between haves and have-nots is pervasive, just as R.K. Merton predicted. What can you and I do as *individuals* to provide countervailing measures and make a difference when billions of dollars in government programs have barely made a dent in the problem? How can we make sense of Cumulative Advantage as a force for good? How do we create an opportunity where there can be momentum for all of us?

## IT BEGINS WITH A SPARK

If you have an open mind and a caring heart, it's impossible to be unaffected by the cycle of despair in the world. This is a staggering and chronic problem that I cannot solve in this or any book.

But I do have an idea.

We know that the momentum of Cumulative Advantage begins with a spark—that initial seed of potential. Maybe the world needs you and I to be in the business of providing sparks.

Cumulative Advantage does not necessarily have to begin with money in the bank, a private prep school education, or access to celebrity influencers. A spark can be an open door, an open heart, or guidance at the right moment in life. Isn't it possible that any person reading this book can provide useful sparks of opportunity to children who need them? Doesn't that just seem ... doable?

Here's a story of hope and "sparks" in action:[6]

Four years ago, things did not look good for Banneker High School in Fulton County, Georgia, about 15 miles south of Atlanta.

It was performing in the bottom 5 percent of all schools in the state. Six out of 10 students did not graduate. Teacher retention was abysmal, and an estimated 97 percent of students lived in poverty. The future for many of the students seemed bleak.

"It just seemed as though there wasn't anything here for kids that would provide a real solution," said Banneker's principal, Dr. Duke Bradley. "School—the very place created to build opportunity and hope—was actually fueling this epidemic. The community had lost confidence in the school."

Fast-forward to 2019 and things at Banneker are very, very different. The graduation rate has increased by 47 percent—the highest growth in the graduation rate among all public high schools in Fulton County. And, in less than two years, Banneker dropped off the state's failing school list and is no longer eligible for state intervention.

"When I walk the halls, I can feel it," Dr. Bradley said. "There is pride."

What caused this breathtaking turnaround? It wasn't due to any windfall of money, buildings, or new staff members. This troubled school turned around because it had an enormous infusion of sparks created by everyday people that led to a redistribution of hope and esteem.

In 2013, the Fulton County school system entered into an agreement with volunteers from the Junior Achievement organization to reimagine what education could be for at-risk teens. This included re-engineering the school structure, curriculum design, and teacher development in a way that would integrate real-life career preparation with a reinforcing high school experience. The initiative was named 3DE, and Banneker High School was selected for the initial pilot in 2015.

Under the 3DE approach, students receive real-life business case challenges and are guided by experienced mentors from sponsoring companies. For example, students might be asked to come up with a solution to help Delta Air Lines improve the boarding process or to support a cybersecurity firm in expanding the use of its simulated training program.

The high school teachers then weave that challenge into the everyday curriculum—from geometry to language studies—to create a meaningful interdisciplinary approach. The students can see how classroom learning is applied in the real world and real jobs.

Students learn the principles of leadership, collaboration, complex problem solving, and skills to navigate conflict as they debate and defend their ideas. At the end of the project, the volunteers hear presentations from the top teams and offer feedback and coaching.

By their senior year, students have completed 16 case challenges with a variety of mentors, and they move on to a year-long immersion project, which could be a consulting assignment, field research, or a paid internship with a local business.

This is a story of progress and hope:

- 3DE students outperform their school peers on 100 percent of key academic benchmarks.
- Chronic absenteeism has fallen by 38 percent.
- Participants have a 92 percent graduation rate compared to 63 percent when the program started.
- There is an 81 percent reduction in disciplinary problems.
- 88 percent of the students enroll in college, far above the national average of 65 percent.

3DE plans to expand to 500 schools by 2030, with an ultimate goal of 2,500 locations (about 10 percent of the U.S. population).

But here is the statistic that made my heart skip a beat: **98 percent of the student participants say they are "excited by their future."** They have esteem.

Poverty is not destiny. "It doesn't work to pity kids raised in poverty and assume that their background dooms them to failure," says Eric Jensen in his landmark book *Teaching with Poverty in Mind*. "What works is to acknowledge that the human brain is designed to *change from experiences* and if we design enough high-quality experiences, over time we will get positive change."

Through our time together, we've learned about the awesome power of reaching up and creating an aspirational mentoring relationship. But there is also power in *reaching down* and being that mentor who provides experiences, opportunities, and connections to those in the undertow.

I am in no way minimizing the extraordinarily complex, systemic problems defining the opportunity gap in America and beyond. But as I've struggled to consider what an individual can reasonably do to have any impact, I don't think we can underestimate the power of creating sparks through mentorship.

Perhaps this is the ultimate grassroots countervailing process. Don't just lend a hand; *be the hand* and help those in this world who are being left behind. As Gloria Nolan said, *the people need to do the work.*

## THE RAINDROP MATTERS

I wanted to end our time together with a message of hope and assurance of the power in your own small contribution to what seems like an overpowering problem. My mind kept coming back to my favorite story from my book KNOWN. It's a true story told by Diana Krahn, an extraordinary woman who has devoted her life to lifting others from poverty and oppression:

> For much of my life I was convicted to help others. As a child I worked side by side with Mother Teresa in the slums of Calcutta. My parents worked

selflessly for the poor, beginning each day with a question: "What can we do to help others today?" My family founded an orphanage that has nurtured more than a hundred children in India.

Serving others was literally seared into my soul. But as an adult, I was afraid to do anything about it. The problems of our world seemed so big, and I was so incredibly small. What could I possibly do to create any kind of meaningful change in the world? And then I remembered an event from when I was a child ...

My aunt worked with Mother Teresa for many years. I would visit my aunt in the slums of Calcutta and I would work right alongside her. When I met Mother Teresa for the first time, I was just 8 years old. So I didn't see her in the way that adults would, I guess. I saw her as this very caring, wonderful, elderly lady who just genuinely loved the poor.

Perhaps she was the most authentic person I've ever met. She wasn't simply a saint in front of the TV cameras or when speaking before the United Nations. She was precisely the same person everywhere ... behind closed doors, to the poorest of the poor, and to me. That was the most touching and inspiring thing to witness.

Of course the shock of stepping from a life of privilege into abject poverty when I visited Mother Teresa was a dizzying sensation. I was a little girl! What could I do to help? There were so many people who needed so much! I was overcome by the immensity of the poverty, the grime, and suffering. What difference could I possibly make?

Mother Teresa sensed my internal struggle. I suppose my reaction was probably quite common to almost everyone who entered her world for the first time.

She took me aside, bent down and said to me in her gentle voice, "Diana, you seem so overwhelmed. And you seem so fascinated by how it all works and you want to help. But you see, I started very small. Everything good and great starts as something small.

Whatever change happens in the world normally begins with little acts. Start with the small kindness. Just care for people. Love people. Stop judging others. When you judge people, you don't have time to love them. So it doesn't matter who they are, or where they're from, or what they look like, just reach out to them. Maybe one act of kindness seems unimportant when there's so much suffering. Maybe you feel like one raindrop in an ocean of need. But even the ocean is not complete without that single raindrop. Just care. Just love. Just take one step. The raindrop matters."

I cannot imagine a better way to end this book. Just care. Just love. Just take one step. We can make a difference. We can.

And, oh yes ... Elijah. For many years my primary mentoring goal was to help him find his own spark of initiative. I wanted to expose him to anything that might create momentum. We went to art festivals and music events, museums, hikes in the woods and treks through big cities. I even bought him an electronic keyboard because he and his brothers showed some musical talent. You never know!

Elijah's Cumulative Advantage was created through his determination, work ethic, and incredible athletic ability. He is an elite athlete, and while I take absolutely no credit for that, I did throw footballs with him until my arm was ready to drop off, and after attending nearly all his games since the fifth grade, I felt I earned that big tear rolling down my cheek when he was named "Mr. Football"—the high school player of the year for our state. He is now attending a major university on a full scholarship. Supported by an extended family with boundless pride and love, the kid has his shot.

Everything good and great starts with something small. What can you do to create sparks of momentum in your part of the world?

At *businessesGROW.com/cumulativeadvantage* I've provided a list of resources that have been vetted by a panel of social responsibility professionals. These organizations have been selected for you because they provide countervailing measures for underprivileged children and shift momentum in our world.

I know there are unending demands on your time, but my humble request is that you visit at least one website listed on this web page. Look around and see if there is a way for you to not just lend a hand but be the hand that changes the momentum for a child, in your city or beyond.

Thank you for reading my book. If you've made it this far, you are a special person and I am grateful for your time and attention. Please keep in touch, and create some sparks, won't you?

# KEEP LEARNING

The topic of Cumulative Advantage and momentum is endlessly fascinating!

I have several options on my website to help you keep learning about this subject and take action. Everything can be found at *www.businessesGROW.com/CumulativeAdvantage.*

- As I mentioned in Chapter 10, I've provided a list of vetted resources where you can learn about organizations creating real, positive momentum for those being left behind.

- I also have a link to relevant blog posts I'm writing on the subject of momentum as I continue to learn about this subject.

- Finally, there is a free chapter summary and study guide to help you think through the ideas from this book and develop your own plan to build momentum for your ideas.

# ACKNOWLEDGEMENTS

In Chapter 3, I tell the story of how Leonard DaVinci's creativity and greatest works were sparked through constant collaboration with friends. Here is my DaVinci Team for *Cumulative Advantage*!

There is no way to sufficiently express the degree to which this book was a true team project. I am exceptionally proud of that and honored that I had the chance to weave so many diverse ideas into a cohesive narrative.

The reigning Captain of my DaVinci Team is **Keith Reynold Jennings**. In 2019, I sent him a couple rough and clunky chapters and asked him, "Is this a book?" He emphatically said "YES," and here we are. Keith also acted as a personal therapist during the times this book had me twisted up like a sick pretzel.

About a year before the writing started, I met **Evelyn Starr** in person for the first time and immediately recognized that I would need her massive intelligence, insight, and experience on board for *Cumulative Advantage*. Her wisdom is deeply embedded here.

There were other significant advisors on this project who made the content richer and more inclusive:

- **Alexandra Kunish** is an Instructor of Professional Practice at the outstanding Rutgers University Business School. She is also Chairperson of the Rutgers Marketing Advisory Board, of which I am proud to be a member.

- **Taneasha White** served as a sensitivity reader to spot cultural inaccuracies, representation issues, bias, stereotypes, and problematic language.

- **Gloria Nolan** is a personal hero. She is a community leader and civil rights activist who has mentored me and encouraged me to dig deep and do the work.

- **Samantha Stone** is the founder of The Marketing Advisory Network who supervised the original research in this book.

- **John Esperian** claims to be a "relentlessly helpful" wordsmith … and he was that to the nth degree. He helped add an international sensibility to the book.

I'm also grateful to **Mitchell Slater** for wise guidance, **Wendy Laman** for keeping me grounded in the real world, **Fabio Tambosi** of Adidas for his constant inspiration, **Elizabeth Sosnow** of Bliss Integrated Communication for generous friendship when I needed it most, and **Jennifer McClellan** for helping this book fly into the world.

My production team includes researcher **Mandy Edwards**, editor **Elizabeth Rea**, designer **Kelly Exeter**, and audio editor **Becky Nieman**.

When writing a book, I become obsessed and somewhat unpleasant. Every day, and in every word, I picture you (yes, YOU!), and I think, "I cannot let them down." I have to deliver something worthy of your time ... a book that is beautiful, bold, and filled with truth and hope.

In this obsessive writing mode, my promise to you thunders in my head for months. I fall asleep with it, dream of it, and wake up remembering things I need to do to make the book even better. The patient curator of my life in this semi-zombie state is **my wife Rebecca**. She is more than enduring and understanding. She enables my vision.

If you made it this far, you are a truly remarkable person, and I intend to reward you. This book has a rather cryptic dedication at the beginning: "To the Parker family ..." I will explain this to you, my intrepid reader of Acknowledgments.

For 13 years I have been closely connected to a woman named Patsy Parker and her life raising five, and sometimes seven, grandchildren by herself. I share a little of her story and that of her grandson Elijah in Chapter 10, but it cannot capture her existence of relentless exhaustion, sacrifice, and infinite strength.

My wife and I started out as "mentors" to Patsy's grandkids, and we try to help where we can. But "mentor" is an insufficient word—the Parkers have become part of our family. I've received ten times the love and inspiration from them compared to what they have ever received from me.

I hope you will consider creating sparks of initial advantage yourself by becoming involved in mentoring in your community. A good place to start is *www.businessesgrow.com/CumulativeAdvantage*.

All my gifts come from God. My prayer is that this book has glorified Him in some small way.

# ABOUT THE AUTHOR

Mark W. Schaefer is a globally-recognized keynote speaker, college educator, marketing consultant, and author.

His blog {grow} is one of the top marketing blogs of the world. Mark's Marketing Companion podcast is among the top 1 percent of all business shows on iTunes.

Mark has worked in global sales, PR, and marketing positions for more than 30 years and now provides consulting services as Executive Director of U.S.-based Schaefer Marketing Solutions. He specializes in marketing training and strategy with clients as diverse as Dell, Johnson & Johnson, Adidas, and the U.S. Air Force.

Mark also serves as Chief Operating Officer at B Squared Media, the premier source for online customer care and digital advertising strategy and management.

He has advanced degrees in marketing and organizational development and is a faculty member of the graduate studies program at Rutgers University. A career highlight was studying under Peter Drucker while earning his MBA.

Mark is among the world's most recognized marketing authorities and has been a keynote speaker at many conferences around the world including The American Bar Association, National Economic Development Association, the Institute for International and European Affairs, and Word of Mouth Marketing Summit Tokyo.

You can stay connected with Mark at *www. BusinessesGROW.com* and by following his adventures on Instagram and Twitter: @markwschaefer

# ENDNOTES

## INTRODUCTION

1   Business Insider podcast "Success! How I Did It" episode: "The 4-Hour Workweek" author Tim Ferriss reveals what he's learned after a difficult year of introspection and how he built a passionate fanbase of millions.

## CHAPTER 1

1   Much of the background information on the secretive Porcellian Club comes from one extraordinary article. Sedgwick, John. "Brotherhood of the Pig." GQ: Gentlemen's Quarterly 58, Nov. 1988.

2   O'Gorman, James F. The Makers of Trinity Church in the City of Boston. University of Massachusetts Press, 2004.

3   Fitzgerald, Maggie. "Zuckerberg reportedly held talks with Winklevoss twins about Facebook's cryptocurrency plans." CNBC website, 24 May 2019.

4   As early as 1942, Merton was writing that the stratification of science involves "the accumulation of differential advantages for certain segments of the population." Merton, Robert K. "The Normative Structure of Science." The Sociology of Science: Theoretical and Empirical Investigations, Ed. Norman Storer. University of Chicago Press, 1973.

5   While later publishing an anthology of his work, Robert Merton confessed that Dr. Zuckerman should have been

named as a co-author of the famous "Matthew Effect" paper. I want to give a proper acknowledgment to the work of Dr. Zuckerman, who is still active at Columbia University and was generous in helping me with the research for this book. Robert Merton's most ironic oversight inspired Margaret Rossiter, a historian of women in science, to coin the term "Matilda Effect," or the pervasive minimizing or neglect of women's scientific contributions.

6   Zuckerman, Harriet. "Nobel Laureate: Sociological Studies of Scientific Collaboration." Columbia University, 1965.

7   Science, vol. 159, no. 3810, 1968, pp. 56-63.

8   This Bible reference is technically not about material possessions. Most scholars say that in this verse, Jesus is talking about God's children who have spiritual truth and understanding of the word. When they share the truth with others, more shall be given to them. Those that have little truth and share not with others will have it taken away and will have no truth or understanding within them.

9   DiPrete, Thomas A. and Eirich, Gregory M. "Cumulative Advantage as a Mechanism for Inequality: A Review of Theoretical and Empirical Developments." Annual Review of Sociology, vol. 32, 2006.

10  In my book, I tend to use "Matthew Effect" and "Cumulative Advantage" interchangeably, as do many other authors. Dr. Harriett Zuckerman, Dr. Merton's research assistant and later wife, sent me an unpublished paper she created to help with my research and noted that although the concepts are being homogenized as time passes, they are different: "The central idea captured in the Matthew Effect, as Merton noted, is that scientists are inclined, both wittingly and unwittingly, to award more recognition to well-known scientists and less to others for contributions of the same or equivalent importance, while

cumulative advantage refers to the repeated advantaging of those who are already advantaged and thus to increasing disparities in opportunities, performance, and rewards. It includes no assumptions about whether such advantages go disproportionately often to those who deserve them."

11  DiPrete, Thomas A. and Eirich, Gregory M. "Cumulative Advantage as a Mechanism for Inequality: A Review of Theoretical and Empirical Developments." Annual Review of Sociology, vol. 32, 2006, p. 271.

12  Ibid

13  The so-called "Best Seller Effect," as demonstrated with the Oscar awards, involves the influence of visible collective approval on the outcomes of a competition. In his Mind of the Market, Michael Shermer equates the Best Seller Effect with the Matthew Effect and adds that "Marketers know it as cumulative advantage."

14  Petersen, Jung, Yang and Stanley. "Quantitative and empirical demonstration of the Matthew Effect in a study of career longevity." Proceedings of the National Academy of Sciences of the USA, 4 Jan. 2011.

15  Bouton, David. Interview with Dr. Keith Stanovich, "Matthew Effects – Does Reading Make You Smarter?" Children of the Code.org.

16  Gladwell, Malcolm. Outliers. Backbay Books, 2011.

17  Research was conducted using 174 anonymous business owners. About 78% were from the U.S.

## CHAPTER 2

1  Ohannessian, Kevin. "Leadership Hall of Fame: Tim Ferriss, Author of "The 4-Hour Workweek." Fast Company, 20 Jan. 2011.

2  The angioplasty and Nike case studies come from The Click Moment by Frans Johansson. Penguin Publishing Group, Kindle Edition.

3  Kantorovich, Aharon, and Yuval Neeman. "Serendipity as a source of evolutionary progress in science." Studies in History and Philosophy of Science, vol. 20, no. 4, 1989, pp. 505-529.

4  De Hoog, Michiel. "Successful people rarely admit how lucky they were. Here's why they should." The Correspondent, 20 Aug. 2020.

5  Frank, Robert H. Success and Luck. Princeton University Press, 2017

6  Frank, Robert H. "Why Luck Matters More Than You Might Think." The Atlantic, May 2016.

7  Edited transcript from "How Spanx Got Started." INC, https://www.inc.com/sara-blakely/how-sara-blakley-started-spanx.html.

8  Lindstrom, Martin. "Unusual innovations for unusual times." The Lindstrom Report on LinkedIn, 1 Sept. 2020, www.linkedin.com/pulse/unusual-innovations-times-martin-lindstrom.

9  Schaefer, Mark. "Get Ready, Social Scoring Will Change Your Life." 22 Nov. 2020, businessesgrow.com/2010/11/22/get-ready-social-scoring-will-change-your-life.

## CHAPTER 3

1  Denrell, Jerker, Christina Fang, and Sidney G. Winter. "The economics of strategic opportunity." Strategic Management Journal, vol. 24, 2003, pp. 977-990.

2  Heffernan, Margaret. "Leadership in Hard Times." Global Peter Drucker Forum, 2020. Presentation.

3  Dew, Nicholas. "Serendipity and Entrepreneurship." Organization Studies, 2009.

4    D'Alessandro, Carrianne. "He turned a terrifying mistake into a fitness craze." INC Magazine, 20 Oct. 2017.

5    My book Marketing Rebellion: The Most Human Company Wins explores this idea in detail.

## CHAPTER 4

1    "Michael Porter." Wikipedia, https://en.wikipedia.org/wiki/Michael_Porter.

2    Some of the ideas for "the seam" were developed through conversations with my friend and mentor Dr. Milind Lele of the University of Chicago.

3    Bradley, Chris, Martin Hirt, Sara Hudson, Nicholas Northcote, and Sven Smit. ""The Great Acceleration." McKinsey & Company, 14 July 2020. https://www.mckinsey.com/business-functions/strategy-and-corporate-finance/our-insights/the-great-acceleration.

4    "Bloomberg Billionaires Index." Bloomberg.com/billionaires.

5    Stewart, Rebecca. "A smart DTC strategy is helping sales fizz for 'wine in a can' brand Babe." The Drum, 17 Aug. 17, 2020.

6    Mr. Burson's book, The Business of Influence, was published in 2017.

7    Dayman, Lucy. "ikigai: The Japanese Concept of Finding Purpose in Life." Savvy Tokyo, 15 Jan. 2020.

## CHAPTER 5

1    Carlson, Nicholas. "The Real History of Twitter." Business Insider, 13 April 2001.

2    Schaefer, Mark. The Tao of Twitter. McGraw-Hill Education, 2011.

3    Gross, Bill. "The single biggest reason why start-ups succeed." YouTube, uploaded by TED, 1 June 2015, www.youtube.com/watch?v=bNpx7gpSqbY.

4   Christensen, Clayton M. The Innovator's Dilemma (Management of Innovation and Change). Kindle ed., Harvard Business Review Press, 2015.

5   Peters, Tom. "Tom Peters's True Confession." Fast Company, 30 Nov. 2001.

6   Gross, Bill. "The single biggest reason why start-ups succeed." YouTube, uploaded by TED, 1 June 2015, www.youtube.com/watch?v=bNpx7gpSqbY.

7   The Lean Startup by Eric Ries is a great resource to explore this idea.

8   Mead, Rebecca. "Better, Faster, Stronger." The New Yorker, 29 August 2011.

9   For a simply fascinating account of Napoleon Hill and his misadventures, I highly recommend "The Untold Story of Napoleon Hill, the Greatest Self-Help Scammer of All Time" by Matt Novack, Gizmodo, 6 Dec. 2016.

## CHAPTER 6

1   The Giro case study was inspired by a story in "Turning the Flywheel," a monograph written by Good to Great author Jim Collins in 2019.

2   "Marketing clout of social media." YouTube, uploaded by CBS, 26 March 2012, www.youtube.com/watch?v=2GHO0bbJrq4.

3   Mead, Rebecca. "Better, Faster, Stronger." The New Yorker, 29 Aug. 2011.

4   Ferriss, Tim. "How to create a global phenomenon with less than $10,000." YouTube, uploaded by LeWeb

5   Salganik, Matthew, Duncan Watts, and Peter Dodds. "Experimental Study of Inequality and Unpredictability in an Artificial Cultural Market." Science, 10 Feb. 2006.

6   Watts, Duncan. "Is Justin Timberlake a Product of Cumulative Advantage?" The New York Times Magazine, 15 Apr. 2007.

## CHAPTER 7

1   Merton, Robert K. "A Life of Learning." Charles Homer Haskins Prize Lecture, 1994.

2   "A happy warrior: Mellody Hobson on mentorship, diversity, and feedback." McKinsey Global Institute, 18 June 2020, www. mckinsey.com/featured-insights/diversity-and-inclusion/a-happy-warrior-mellody-hobson-on-mentorship-diversity-and-feedback. Edited podcast transcript.

3   "How To Attract The Best Mentors, According to Tim Ferriss." Entrepreneur, 21 Nov. 2017, www.entrepreneur. com/video/304995. Video blog with Jason Feifer.

## CHAPTER 8

1   Cured. Directed by Joe York, 2012.www.southernfoodways. org/film/cured. Edited transcript.

2   Some of the information in this section was inspired by the article "Changing How We Think About Change" by Hunsaker, Ettenson and Knowles, MIT Sloan Management Review, 13 Aug. 2020. sloanreview.mit.edu/article/changing-how-we-think-about-change/. This is an excellent resource when applying Cumulative Advantage to a business setting.

3   There are lots of articles on this subject, but a good summary is from Dr. Benjamin Hardy, "How to Rewrite Your Past Narrative." Psychology Today, 26 July 2019.

4   Samuels, Doug. "Nick Saban breaks down what 'The Process' really is, and where his belief in it began." Football Scoop, 31 Jan. 2018, footballscoop.com/news/nick-saban-breaks-process-really-belief-began/.

5   Duckworth, Angela. Grit: The Power of Passion and Perseverance. Collins, 2016.

## CHAPTER 10

1   An interesting resource on this topic is the film "No No," a documentary about Pirate pitcher Dock Ellis and racial issues in Pittsburgh during this time frame.

2   Coman, Julian. "Michael Sandel: 'The populist backlash has been a revolt against the tyranny of merit.'" The Observer, 6 Sept. 2020, www.theguardian.com/books/2020/sep/06/michael-sandel-the-populist-backlash-has-been-a-revolt-against-the-tyranny-of-merit.

3   Hess, Abigail. "Rich students get better SAT scores—here's why." MSNBC, 19 Oct. 2019, www.cnbc.com/2019/10/03/rich-students-get-better-sat-scores-heres-why.html.

4   Jensen, Eric. Teaching with Poverty in Mind: What Being Poor Does to Kids' Brains and What Schools Can Do About It. ASCD Press, 2009.

5   Ip, Greg. "For African-Americans, a Painful Economic Reversal of Fortune." The Wall Street Journal, 3 June 2020, www.wsj.com/articles/for-african-americans-a-painful-economic-reversal-of-fortune-11591176602.

6   Kohn, Maggie. "Businesses and Educators Come Together to Transform the High School Experience." TriplePundit, 9 Sept. 2019, www.triplepundit.com/story/2019/businesses-and-educators-come-together-transform-high-school-experience/84821.

# INDEX